One of
Churchill's Own

This book is dedicated to the Pilots of Battle of Britain Squadron No 253: Hyderabad Squadron. Royal Air Force.

"Come one, Come all"

One of
Churchill's Own

The Memoirs of Battle of
Britain Pilot John Greenwood

John Greenwood

Pen & Sword
AVIATION

First published in Great Britain in 2016 by
Pen & Sword Aviation
an imprint of
Pen & Sword Books Ltd
47 Church Street
Barnsley
South Yorkshire
S70 2AS

ISBN 978 1 47387 267 7

Typeset in Ehrhardt by
Mac Style Ltd, Bridlington, East Yorkshire
Printed and bound in the UK by CPI Group (UK) Ltd,
Croydon, CRO 4YY

Pen & Sword Books Ltd incorporates the imprints of Pen &
Sword Archaeology, Atlas, Aviation, Battleground, Discovery,
Family History, History, Maritime, Military, Naval, Politics,
Railways, Select, Transport, True Crime, and Fiction, Frontline
Books, Leo Cooper, Praetorian Press, Seaforth Publishing and
Wharncliffe.

For a complete list of Pen & Sword titles please contact
PEN & SWORD BOOKS LIMITED
47 Church Street, Barnsley, South Yorkshire, S70 2AS, England
E-mail: enquiries@pen-and-sword.co.uk
Website: www.pen–and–sword.co.uk

Contents

Glossary

AOC	Air Officer Commanding
BAFO	British Air Forces of Occupation
CFI	Chief Flying Instructor
CFO	Chief Flying Officer (not widely used, but John references it)
CO	Commanding Officer
DFC	Distinguished Flying Cross
DSO	Distinguished Service Order
E & RFTS	Elementary and Reserve Flying Training School
FANY	First Aid Nursing Yeomanry
F/L	Flight Lieutenant
F/O	Flying Officer
F/Sgt	Flight Sergeant
FTS	Flying Training School
HMS	His Majesty's Ship
HQ	Headquarters
IAF	Indian Air Force
IFF	Identification Friend or Foe
LNER	London and North Eastern Railway
MC	Military Cross
MM	Military Medal
MP	Military Police
NCO	Non-Commissioned Officer
OTU	Operational Training Unit

P/O	Pilot Officer
POW	Prisoner Of War
RAAF	Royal Australian Air Force
RAE	Royal Aircraft Establishment
RCAF	Royal Canadian Air Force
Sgt	Sergeant
S/L	Squadron Leader
VC	Victoria Cross
WAAF	Women's Auxiliary Air Force

Prologue: Lille Marque, France, 17 May 1940

The first night we slept in a tent because there was no other accommodation for us. We were freezing cold, just lying on stretchers in our flying gear with one blanket and nothing else, so we got very little sleep at all. The next morning we got up early. I was standing in the mist and cold when I saw two Lysanders, Army Co-op machines making their final approach to land. Suddenly, four Me109's came from nowhere, I remember no sound whatsoever before the attack then off they went again, while both Lysanders dived straight into the ground, going up in a huge burst of flame. I can remember no sound because I was in a state of shock, I guess. This was my initiation into air warfare and I realised that this was war and it was deadly serious.

Foreword

by Michael Greenwood

My father was 69 years old when I first hugged him and while the action felt strange at the time it was a cathartic experience for me; expressing my love for a man I had only ever shook hands with in the past.

During the war, Dad enjoyed the company of his fellow brothers in arms but never formed close friendships because death stalked them all and to lose a close friend was emotionally draining. Combined with the distant relationship he experienced with his own father, I believe an in-built defensive mechanism led to the lack of physical affection towards his children during childhood.

In July 1981, on my maiden travel adventure to Europe, I met my Uncle Bob, the husband of Dad's younger sister Ruth, a learned man with a history of working for the US diplomatic core who spoke of Dad as a hero. Up until then, I had only ever recognised Dad as my loving father. Bob confirmed Dad's hero status by explaining his brave actions during the Battle of France, Battle of Britain and on Catapult Ships. It was then that I privately recognised his bravery and he became my hero too.

This realisation was fulfilled ten years later as I stood in the Mall in London with thousands of other people, all watching a wonderful flypast of modern military aircraft, preceded by four Spitfires and two Hurricanes. Standing not 300 metres from Buckingham Palace, were Mum and Dad, sat in the forecourt with many other Battle of Britain pilots and wives; there was a lull in proceedings before I heard this low rumbling sound of two powerful engines approaching me at speed. The noise grew louder until it came to a crescendo and I received the full engine blasts of a Hurricane and Spitfire, wingtip to wingtip, in formation, at treetop level and hurtling down the Mall towards Buckingham Palace; the Hurricane broke left and the Spitfire right, splitting around the Palace while each performed a victory roll – the hairs on the back of my neck were standing on end. In that moment tears came to my eyes; I felt so proud of my father who, as a young man, had flown a Hurricane against a deadly enemy both in France and then during the Battle of Britain. My father never regarded himself anything other than a working class man who performed his duty. He abhorred the carnage of active duty so any wartime stories he told the family were of a humorous nature. In this book you will read the story of a young man who lost his youth to war. During the post-war years he was annoyed and disappointed with successive governments who ordered servicemen overseas on active service.

The man my family knew as Dad loved the company of other people. He enjoyed sharing stories and jokes and accepted everyone on the same level from dignitaries and high-level businessmen to the common battler. He stood up for the underdog, disliked snobbery and pompousness, thumbed his nose at authority and was not afraid to communicate his opinion. Most of all, I loved his irreverent sense of humour.

Behind every good man there is a very, very good woman. In Dad's case this has been Joyce. The relationship went within an ace of disintegrating well before it ever had a chance to bloom. In the early 1950s dad was a pilot, a first officer with an Australian commercial airline and mum was a hostess. They met and were attracted to one another and after a short courting period they married in January 1954 and the Greenwood clan from Western Australia began.

Dad always questioned authority where he saw the need. In the early 1950s, flying for an airline based out of Adelaide, he felt that pilots, not just in his airline, but in the industry as a whole, were being made to fly aircraft dangerously overloaded with freight.

Airline management refused to listen to Dad when he raised the issue of reducing loads by at least 1,000 lbs. Experience during the war had taught him that if enough individuals banded together, they had the power to affect change. He convened an off-site meeting of the captains and first officers, including pilots flying for another airline company, and sought their support in enforcing airlines not to exceed acceptable cargo weight limits, thereby ensuring the safety of the aircraft and those who flew them. The strike lasted one week before the aviation authority flew an aircraft up to a reasonable height with the weight the airline were expecting pilots to carry. One engine was cut and the aircraft lost height quickly. Following this result a law was passed that the airlines must drop the weight limit by 2,000 lbs. The airline concerned subsequently branded Dad and a few others as 'troublemakers' and when he missed his roster, they saw an opportunity to terminate his employment along with several others. They also made sure that the tag of 'troublemaker' stuck, making it impossible for Dad to find other employment within the close-knit Australian aviation industry. In his early thirties, his career in the thing he loved to do most was prematurely over; ruined by men who valued profit over human life. The loss he felt for not being able to fly in Australia again hurt him deeply. Giving the airline the excuse to sack him is the only regret he ever had in life, but he remained proud that he stood up to corporate bullies.

When Dad purchased a newsagents in the Western Australian country town of Gnowangerup, he not only found a business but, as my younger brother Nick expressed in his eulogy, *he found a home*. Dad loved the close-knit community and the reliance on one another for work and play. He loved the people he met there – many of whom remained friends for the rest of their lives. His closest friend in the town, Keith Richardson, had been a pilot during the Second World War and they could relate to each other's experiences with a shared bond of humour. In the town Dad was his own boss and, finally, he controlled his own destiny.

In September 1965 Dad returned to the UK for the first time in fifteen years when the RAF offered free travel for ex-Battle of Britain pilots to attend the 25th Anniversary of the battle. Dad accepted the offer while Mum ran the business and looked after their four young children. At the reunion he met many of his old 253 Squadron mates including his squadron leader and good friend Tom Gleave. This anniversary was very special to Dad because it was the first gathering of his old squadron and others since those terrible days back in 1940. The numbers of veterans attending dwindled with the commemoration of each subsequent anniversary.

In 1973 when Dad decided to sell his business and move the family to Safety Bay, he made the conscious choice to sell it to his loyal long-term employee, Gwen, rather than accept a higher outside bidder. He allowed her to repay some of it over time through the cash flow of the business because she could not raise all the finance required in advance. That decision to put loyalty over money was, in his mind, the right thing to do.

Dad worked as a sales representative for Tubemakers Australia based in Kwinana Western Australia for the following seven years and mum started working again to ensure the children received a good education. At 60 years of age he retired and enjoyed every day of his 'freedom'. Reading books, painting, watching films, walking his dog, discussions about anything as he was very well read. He always had an opinion about politics; talking about cricket especially when the Ashes Series came around; Aussies Rules football, soccer as he was an Arsenal Fan – to name just a few topics. Playing golf and playing bowls consumed the rest of his time. In his seventies Dad was diagnosed with acute Diverticulitis. He was in constant pain but would not have an operation which meant wearing a colostomy bag. Fortunately he found a surgeon who could perform an operation where the intestines could be attached to what was left of the bowel and by going ahead he ensured his quality of life was extended and he bounced back pain free. During these years he dictated his war memories on to tape which Mum diligently compiled into a manuscript which formed the basis for this book.

In 1980 Dad and Mum travelled to the UK for the 40th anniversary of the Battle of Britain where he met up with his two sisters, Betty and Ruth, for the first time in decades. In September 1990 the RAAF flew all ex-Battle of Britain pilots and their partners over to the UK for the 50th anniversary. It was a massive event involving formal dinners each night and Dad enjoyed being reunited with old friends. His sister Betty was present (she had married an ex-Battle of Britain pilot), our cousin Dave (the son of Dad's sister Ruth) and his wife Karen; Melody (Ruth's daughter); My sister Helen, brother Nicholas and myself all went with Dad organising tickets for most of us to attend the service in Westminster Abbey. As an extended family we shared a house for five days not far from the town of Farnham and enjoyed the most wonderful get-together.

Dad and Mum returned to the UK again in 2000 for the 60th anniversary commemorations. There were only a few of 253 Squadron pilots form the Battle of Britain still alive one of them being his mate

'Corky' whom he had not seen for decades and they enjoyed a happy lunch together with family following the commemoration ceremony at Westminster Abbey. It proved to be the last time they saw one another. He also met up with Guy Harris the 253 Squadron Flight Commander of B Flight who was shot down and badly injured during the Battle of France. Due to his injuries he did not take an active role in the Battle of Britain but Dad always obtained tickets for him to attend the annual services at Westminster Abbey.

In 2005 Dad and Mum travelled to London for the last time. On this occasion Dad was on hand to witness the opening of the Battle of Britain monument located on the Embankment. At the unveiling Prince Charles stopped and had a quick chat to Dad about cricket, which he enjoyed.

In 1999 I established a web site based on Dad's Battle of Britain experience which was later taken over by the Battle of Britain Historical Society. Through the Guestbook application on the website, Dad corresponded with hundreds of interested people over the ensuing years and it helped him establish close relationships with like-minded individuals connected to the Battle of Britain Society. He enjoyed replying to families of his 253 Squadron comrades, helping them to understand more about their relative's experiences. Through the site he received information about the restoration of a Hurricane aircraft which he had actually flown back in 1940 as recorded in his Log Book. He was very interested in the restoration, not so much because he had flown the aircraft, but more because it represented a working memorial to his beloved 253 Squadron members of which he was, by then, the last surviving member. In 2013, along with my two brothers Chris and Nick, I witnessed first-hand the restoration progress of the Hurricane on a farm in the UK county of Suffolk. The plan is for the Hurricane to fly again sometime during 2016.

The last time I hugged my father was in October 2014 outside the family home in Safety Bay before I flew back to my home in Sydney. We both knew this was going to be our last embrace as his health was failing and his will to live was all but extinguished. I held Dad, who was now a frail 93-year-old, and I didn't want to let go. As we released our hold I wanted to say I loved him but I would have broken down in the audience of my wife and mother – this would not do. Dad knew though as I saw a tear in his eye.

In January 2015 Dad's funeral attracted a gathering of around ninety people; not bad for an old man who had outlived most of his friends over the preceding decades. Our family conducted the ceremony as a celebration of his life – tributes, plenty of laughter and a time to reflect.

During a video interview I conducted with him back in the late 1990s I asked him: "While people were attending your wake and you wanted to leave them with a message, what would you say?" His reply was this: "Do your own thing. If you don't agree with something – say so. Lead your own life and always support the underdog; they need the help."

He lives with our immediate and extended families every day through all the wonderful, mainly humorous memories that keep flooding back.

To finish with, Dad often recited his favourite Shakespearian quotes to the audience of his family and my sister Helen's favourite quote was from *As You Like It*:

All the world's a stage, and all the men and women merely players.
They have their exits and their entrances; and one man in his time
plays many parts.

Our father, Our hero.

Excerpt Winston Churchill's Speech: House of Commons, 20 August 1940.

The great air battle which has been in progress over this Island for the last few weeks has recently attained a high intensity. It is too soon to attempt to assign limits either to its scale or to its duration. We must certainly expect that greater efforts will be made by the enemy than any he has so far put forth. Hostile air fields are still being developed in France and the Low Countries, and the movement of squadrons and material for attacking us is still proceeding. It is quite plain that Herr Hitler could not admit defeat in his air attack on Great Britain without sustaining most serious injury. If after all his boastings and bloodcurdling threats and lurid accounts trumpeted round the world of the damage he has inflicted, of the vast numbers of our Air Force he has shot down, so he says, with so little loss to himself; if after tales of the panic-stricken British crushed in their holes cursing the plutocratic Parliament which has led them to such a plight – if after all this his whole air onslaught were forced after a while tamely to peter out, the Fuhrer's reputation for veracity of statement might be seriously impugned. We may be sure, therefore, that he will continue as long as he has the strength to do so, and as long as any preoccupations he may have in respect of the Russian Air Force allow him to do so.

On the other hand, the conditions and course of the fighting have so far been favourable to us. I told the House two months ago that, whereas in France our fighter aircraft were wont to inflict a loss of two or three to one upon the Germans, and in the fighting at Dunkirk, which was a kind of no-man's-land, a loss of about three or four to one, we expected that in an attack on this Island we should achieve a larger ratio. This has certainly come true. It must also be remembered that all the enemy machines and pilots which are shot down over our Island, or over the seas which surround it, are either destroyed or captured; whereas a considerable proportion of our machines, and also of our pilots, are saved, and soon again in many cases come into action.

A vast and admirable system of salvage, directed by the Ministry of Aircraft Production, ensures the speediest return to the fighting line of damaged machines, and the most provident and speedy use of all the spare parts and material. At the same time the splendid – nay, astounding – increase in the output and repair of British aircraft and engines which Lord Beaverbrook has achieved by a genius of organisation and drive, which looks like magic, has given us overflowing reserves of every type of aircraft, and an ever-mounting stream of production both in quantity and quality. The enemy is, of course, far more numerous than we are. But our new production already, as I am advised, largely exceeds his, and the American production is only just beginning to flow in. It is a fact, as I see from my daily returns, that our bomber and fighter strength now, after all this fighting, are larger than they have ever been. We believe that we shall be able to continue the air struggle indefinitely and as long as the enemy pleases, and the longer it continues the more rapid will be our approach, first towards that parity, and then into that superiority, in the air upon which in a large measure the decision of the war depends.

The gratitude of every home in our Island, in our Empire, and indeed throughout the world, except in the abodes of the guilty, goes out to the British airmen who, undaunted by odds, unwearied in their constant challenge and mortal danger, are turning the tide of the World War by their prowess and by their devotion. **Never in the field of human conflict was so much owed by so many to so few.** *All hearts* *go out to the fighter pilots, whose brilliant actions we see with our own eyes day after day; but we must never forget that all the time, night after night, month after month, our bomber squadrons travel far into Germany, find their targets in the darkness by the highest navigational skill, aim their attacks, often under the heaviest fire, often with serious loss, with deliberate careful discrimination, and inflict shattering blows upon the whole of the technical and war-making structure of the Nazi power. On no part of the Royal Air Force does the weight of the war fall more heavily than on the daylight bombers, who will play an invaluable part in the case of invasion and whose unflinching zeal it has been necessary in the meanwhile on numerous occasions to restrain.*

Chapter 1

Early Years

I was born on 3 April, 1921, in Stratford in the East End of London, the middle child of three, having a sister on each side. My eldest sister was Betty and my younger one Ruth. Betty is still alive living in the North of Scotland; her retired Bank Manager husband Noel (and ex Battle of Britain Pilot) having died a few years ago. Ruth, my younger sister, died a few years ago of a brain tumour. I wept when I heard the news for she and I remained soul mates although I didn't see her for thirty-five years after the war because I left for Australia and she for America and many other countries with her husband Bob, who was a diplomat in the service of the United States of America.

My mother and father were normal people. Mum was full of fun, always up to telling jokes and funny stories about her family. While my father was a little more serious, did not smoke and drank very little. Betty was two years older than me but acted more like ten as she too was of a very serious nature and religiously reported all my misadventures (which were many) to my parents, resulting in painful punishment from my father. Needless to say she was not my favourite sister. When I was seven, we both contracted scarlet fever and were sent to the isolation hospital at Isleworth, some ten miles from our home. Betty loved being in hospital and determined, then and there, to be a nurse when she grew up. Betty was often left to look after my sister Ruth and myself when my parents went out but Ruth and I gave her a very hard time. To this day she still bears a small scar on her forehead from a teaspoon that I threw at her.

In later life when I came to Australia we lost touch, never having much in common, but this was corrected during my visit to the UK in 1980 and we keep in touch regularly by telephone. We have met twice since, in England in 1990 and again in 2000 when she visited us in Perth, Western Australia where I now live. She has two children, a son and a daughter.

My other sister Ruth and I were always the greatest of friends. We got up to all sorts of mischief together and often had midnight feasts with food and drinks stolen from the larder. On one such night we were having a feast by the light of a candle when we heard our father coming up the stairs so we quickly hid the food under the bed, accidentally setting alight the tassels from the bedspread. Putting the fire out with my hands (so I thought) we rapidly retired from the scene of the crime and went to our bedrooms. The next thing, there was a cry from my father when he saw that the bedroom was in a sheet of flame. The bedclothes and the mattress were on fire so he grabbed them and threw them out through the window, where they were extinguished and eventually thrown away. Knowing that I would soon receive the thrashing of my life, I went into the spare room and locked myself inside. I was threatened and coerced all that night and the next day until my mother, nearly hysterical, made a solemn promise that I would not be beaten by my father, I then came out after twenty-four hours of solitary confinement. While my sister Ruth got off scot-free!

We never met Dad's mother and father because they died before we were born but he had two sisters and a brother, who we did meet, and some others we did not. One sister, Martha was a housekeeper for a rich family at Byfleet, so rich they owned two cars, a Packard and a Willys Knight. Ruth and I hated her because she had a huge, enormous brown mole with whiskers like wire sticking on the side of her mouth. This wouldn't have been too bad if she hadn't insisted on kissing us with the wettest mouth I have ever been kissed with. Even that would have been bearable if she had given us sixpence or a shilling when she left; but the best she ever did was a peppermint which she found in her bag and had had since 1066! Dad's other sister Carrie lived at Southend and there was something odd about her husband – though we never did find out what because nobody talked about him. Anyway, in 1931 Dad became very ill with shingles and he had scabs all over his head and right around his belly. Mum was so worried that she arranged for us to stay at Aunty Carrie's. Dad took us by car to Fenchurch Street Station, put us onto the train and Aunty Carrie met us at Southend in the afternoon where we were given stewed prunes with custard and a dose of Castor Oil for tea before being sent to bed. I was in a tiny room on a camp bed, all very new and different from what I had been used to.

That first night was so hot I did not sleep well so got up early and explored. Breakfast was the worst I had ever had; porridge made with water, no sugar, and I couldn't leave the table until it was finished. Both Ruth and I sat there for ages until Aunty Carrie had to answer the door and when she left the room I put a great lump of porridge in my handkerchief and then in my pocket. Poor Ruth did not have a handkerchief and I could not take hers as well so she ended up having to eat it. After breakfast we went down to the seaside which seemed miles away and down onto the pier which went out forever. We got back at the end of the day, hot and tired and I was in a nice old mess as the castor oil had caught up with me and I had forgotten the porridge in my pocket which had melted and added to the mess down my leg. Aunty Carrie cuffed me around the ear – there is no such thing as justice, as it was her fault I did it! The house was the hottest and smelliest that I have ever lived in. On the kitchen table where we ate there was a fly-trap, a wire cage shaped like a globe with zillions of flies buzzing around inside, slowly dying of starvation. I thought it very cruel so I took the cage outside and set them free. You'd have thought I had set the house on fire by the performance that Aunty Carrie put on. I was sent to bed early and could hear Carrie 'phone my Mum; we were sent home next day. Apparently I was to blame but I didn't care even if I got a good hiding when I got home. Mum met us at the station and was so pleased to see us that she forgot to belt me! Dad seemed a little better and on the road to recovery. I couldn't help hoping that Aunty Carrie died of starvation in a trap! Albert was the only other brother that we met, and we only saw him three or four times. He lived on the other side of London to us in Dagenham and worked at the Ford plant. I remember him being in the St John's Ambulance Brigade and having a fetish for keeping all his children's ears clean by pouring olive oil down them. He did this to me on my last visit and spoiled a brand new shirt with his bloody olive oil!

My mother's relatives were much more interesting. Her mother and father were still alive and for the first five years of my life we lived with them at their double fronted shop at Stratford in London E15. Mother had two sisters, the eldest was Gladys who we never met because she had married a Canadian serviceman at the end of the First World War in 1918 and emigrated. They lived in a place called Beaver Lodge on the Peace River north of Edmonton in Alberta. My mother and Gladys wrote to each other at least once a week and mother quite often cried over the letters she received as she read of their poverty and the freezing cold conditions. I don't know what became of them all, but it turns out they were sitting on a great oil field so I hope they did nicely out of it.

My mother's youngest sister Gwen married a clerk in the LNER Railway and lived for a time in nearby Romford, but went north to

York when her husband was promoted. They had two daughters, Doreen, the youngest, was brainy and quiet but her older sister Pat was completely the opposite. It was through her that I learned about the female anatomy playing 'Hospitals'. My grandfather was a real character, as I found out in later years. In those days he used to bounce me up and down on his knees and tell me stories until, when I was 5 years old, he died of cancer. Grandma I remember as being fat and always dressed in black with completely silver hair. A very nice old soul who I almost killed once by accidently dropping a carpet on her head from the third floor!

Before I was born, my Grandfather was a builder and decorator of some standing in the community. Once a month he used to collect rents for homeowners and one particular day he did not come home from his collecting. Instead he went to the Epsom races, arriving home a week later with no money. Consequently, he had to sell his business to pay back all the money he had lost. Fortunately, the business was worth more than his debts and with the balance he bought the double fronted shop that became our home. One side of the shop was his and was filled with clay pipes and fittings and all sorts of plumbers and builders paraphernalia. The other side was Grandma's in which she sold tobacco, snuff and cigarettes. One day, when the postman's bike had a puncture, he asked Grandma if he could put it inside Grandfather's shop until he could repair it. When my grandfather came home from the pub later that night, he stumbled in through the door and hit his shin on the cycle pedal. 'I'll teach that bugger to leave it there,' he said; whereupon he picked up an axe and began chopping the bike up!

Chapter 2

School Years

By the time I was 5 years old our family had moved three times and I had attended four schools. For the first year, I attended a school in the East End of London called Waterlane; then for two years at Orleans School at St Margaret's, Middlesex. When we moved to Tolworth in the southwest of London I attended the Council School until the age of ten. After that I was inducted into Tiffins' Public Secondary school where I remained until I began my working career aged fourteen.

At the first school, Waterlane, I remember being brought home by my teacher because I had been caught chasing small girls around the school yard with a pen-knife. While at the second school, Orleans, Betty and I caught scarlet fever when she was 9 years old and I was 7. We were sent to the isolation hospital at Isleworth, some ten miles from our home. While we were there our parents decided that we might as well have our tonsils out – a very painful operation and one not to be recommended. Whereas Betty loved hospital, I was the opposite and hated my incarceration so much so that I escaped from the ward in my pyjamas. I got into the grounds, climbed over the gates, and was on my way home when, barely half a mile away from the hospital, I was recognised by the postman and recaptured.

At Tolworth I began to play and enjoy sports, mainly cricket and football. Academically, I was capable but never brilliant and only did well in the subjects I liked. It was also the period when my best friend, the traitor, got me into St Matthews', Surbiton Choir. The

Judus was paid one piece of silver in the form of a florin for his efforts by my parents. My final school, Tiffin, was in Kingston-on-Thames and it was this period that I remember particularly clearly. I was there for four years starting in Form 1A which was for the brighter boys, and finishing my career in 4C which was for the less bright boys – a pretty good indication of my dedication to work! I never got into any serious trouble while at school, although I had many minor scrapes and was often detained after school. This was recorded in two pages of my Record Book; there were forty spaces to state the reason for detention and work done while detained. My two pages were usually full before the end of the year – and an additional page was added. Most of the detentions were given by the French and Latin masters, initials TAF which was T.A. Fish and RB which was R. Burgess. I learned that a very good forgery can be attained by copying signatures upside down, so I quite often didn't attend detention, instead I copied the initials of the detention masters before the inspection next period. I am happy to say that I was never found out, because that could have meant expulsion. I only tried hard to learn the subjects I liked; these being geography, history and mathematics. In these subjects I usually finished in the top five while in Physics, Chemistry and English, the bottom five and in Latin and French, absolutely bottom. In my last yearly exams before leaving I got Q0/0 in both subjects and this finally made up my father's mind to put me to work.

In my final year, I played for the 1st Eleven at cricket, the youngest member of the team at 14 and at shooting, I obtained my Surrey Marksmanship Badge. Both of which I obtained my school colours. I also played rugby for the third XV and learned to swim; but it was cricket that was my big love and has always remained so. While they tell you that school was the best years of your life, it wasn't true for me. When I left school the only thing I regretted was not playing cricket and I have never once in my life wished I was back at school!

I remember some of the masters at school by their little foibles. With our woodworking master, Mr Lambert or "Bargee" – and he really did look like a barge, a real big, tough looking chap who was actually a gentle giant, would carefully explain what we were to do. He would then walk about the class inspecting our efforts, every now and then coming across something being done wrongly. If you were the culprit, you would feel your ear being twisted and pulled upwards until you were standing on tiptoes, then came the standard sentence, "This boy has done exactly what I told him not to do". I enjoyed woodwork but used to make so many mistakes that I came away with sore ears! I remember making an egg-stand which was built to hold ten eggs laid by normal chickens. Somehow I must have used the wrong tool, and upon proudly presenting it to my Mum, she promptly placed in an egg which fell through and broke. However, being a loving mother she found that it held duck eggs and, not wishing to hurt me, she bought a dozen. However, if there is one thing I dislike it is a boiled or fried duck egg. When the eggs were finished I 'accidentally' broke the stand, much to everyone's satisfaction.

Our English master was a great round ruddy man known as Tuddenhan, who was very fond of giving the cane on the bottom (four of the best). He did not believe in messing around and, being unable to sit down for several minutes, you certainly knew what had hit you! My worst experience with him was one morning when for some reason I knew that I was in for the high jump; I placed in my pants a thin linen copy of "Montezuma", which we were studying at the time. In due course I was told to bend over, then TWANG, what a noise it made. I had to remove it and was given a double dose for my troubles. I can still feel it! English literature was a great bore since Shakespeare was quite beyond my imagination other than to listen for the rude parts.

Chemistry was one of my worst subjects, yet I enjoyed it as the master was a lovely old gentleman who put up with some terrible things from his pupils, such as putting a boy's head in the poison gas chamber after chlorine had been made. Or attaching long lengths of rubber tubing from a gas tap on the bench, affixing a whistle at the end of the tube and then hiding it in a cupboard a few yards away from the gas tap which was turned off and on at will. The noise came a long way from the source and was very hard to find.

The French master, Taffy Fish, was a really nice old gentleman but he used to fill my Log Book up and made me stay from four to five regularly because I just couldn't do French. It was the same with Latin; Reg Burgess, the Latin master, was a nice chap but I was so poor at Latin that I was always in detention. Reg had a talent for rugby and played for Richmond. Those are the only masters who made any impression on me, the rest were quite forgettable.

I was at Tolworth Council School when I joined the 'Black Gang'. There were six members, the oldest of which was 15 years old and I was their youngest at 9 years old. One of the other boys, Bob Wigsell went to Kingston Grammar School and the other three went to Surbiton County School. By present day standards the things we got up to were quite mild, but in the early 1930s our escapades were considered daring. Between us, we dug through the London clay to create a large hole in the ground, similar to the dug-outs built during the First World War. At that time, all the comics were filled with stories about the war, dug-outs and tanks so we created this big, deep hole with half a dozen steps leading down into the 'dug-out' which had a tin and plywood roof and a large drain pipe sticking up through the roof to let the smoke out. This make-shift chimney was necessary because we used to light a fire in the dug-out and cook potatoes and bacon and whatever we could steal from home. We would also smoke our halfpenny clay pipes filled with tobacco from dog-ends picked up from the footpaths, taking all the old tobacco out from their wrapping which we then put into a tin. Of course, the ventilation was useless. We would sit round the smoking fire with streaming eyes, handkerchiefs out, with visibility of about one to two feet while we waited for our bacon, jacket-potatoes, or whatever we were cooking on the fire.

We built a raft to use on the River Hogsmill – they called it a river, but it was little more than a stream really; about 20 ft wide and a tributary of the Thames. This raft, along with our dug-out, was our main means of defying the establishment until the elders of our tribe planned to rob some of the larger stores in Kingston-on-Thames, namely Woolworths, Marks and Spencers and Bentalls. So one Saturday morning, the six of us, led by the eldest and complete with our school caps (so that there would be no doubt if followed where we came from), toured two of the above stores stealing a variety of goods from electric trains to lollies. Sixty-four years later I can remember quite clearly what my contributions to the fun was, a large blunt scout knife with a thing to take stones out of horses' hooves, a fountain pen (inferior make) and a little balsa wood boat which moved its slow pace on water when a piece of camphor was attached to the rear end. It was only many years later that I understood how it worked, by watching a Cadbury's advertisement with a very eccentric Australian Professor explaining surface tension. As well as the above, I sampled quite a number of lollies. When we arrived back at our underground base I was amazed to see what some of the other boys had pinched, including Hornby electric trains, watches and similar. I thanked the Lord we had not been caught; but that was where I was wrong. From the first store we went in, a detective had spotted us and followed us, making a note of all the culprits.

On Monday morning the detective identified the three boys from Surbiton County who broke down and split on the other three members, of whom I was one. Ken Wilson was another and George Broadbent the third. We found out on Monday night that we were in for the high-jump on Tuesday morning so Ken Wilson and I decided to run away that afternoon. We gathered a few things to eat and started off down the Kingston Bypass towards London. We walked for hours then, cold, tired and hungry, decided we would be better off braving the wrath to come. Our mothers and fathers were beginning to wonder where we were and were about to phone the police.

The next day at school the message that I had been dreading arrived: *Would I please report to the Headmaster's study immediately*. I went on jelly legs, with liquid bowel and a dry mouth into 'the jaws of death '. The Headmaster, Mr Stokoe, informed me that we had been followed and, very surprised that I should be amongst the thieves, asked what I had taken. I was sent home to tell my parents all about it and then to return to Mr Stokoe. The fear of what my father would do to me stopped me from going home, so I spent the morning on the Recreation Ground playing cricket. I went back to school in the afternoon and reported to the Head, very tearfully, that I had told my Mum and that she was taking all the goods back. She also beat me and told me that I was going to get an almighty hiding from my father when he arrived home from work that night. This seemed to go down very well with Mr. Stokoe who admonished me and told me that I had got into bad company, not to do it again and he hoped that this would be a stern lesson for me. At the first opportunity, I buried all the stolen goods in the garden and tried to forgot the matter. Two years later however, my father was talking with Mr Wigsall over the garden fence and he mentioned, in passing, our big thieving expedition of which my father knew nothing until that moment, so eventually retribution caught up with me. I learnt the meaning of fear and promised myself I would never steal again. The main lesson though was that if you do something wrong, don't get found out until it is too late to matter anymore!

Around this time I started to read and enjoy books and learned what awful beasts sisters are. I had just finished a very sad book entitled *Netta's Call* – I'll always remember it beause Netta dies of consumption at the end. I was sobbing my eyes out when Betty came into my room and caught me in full blast. When she found what it was all about she hurried to tell Ruth and now every time they saw me it was "Poor little Netta" or "How's Netta?" and I immediately burst into tears again. I hated them and was determined to get my own back. Soon afterwards, I found Betty's diary in her room. It was unlocked so I read it! She had written a lot in Morse Code (learned at Girl Guides) but I had a code table from the Cubs, most of it was boring until I came to the part that said, 'Should like to get to know GT and TT'. Wow! This was great because Betty was a prude and told on me if I did anything wrong, which was often. Right opposite us lived two brothers, a couple of years older than Betty, their names were Tom Thomas and George Thomas. I told Ruth and every time we saw Betty, we said, "Should like to get to know GT and TT". She burst into tears the first time and told Mum that we had read her diary; but she didn't get much action there.

In my last year at school Mum and Dad forced me to go for a week to Cadet Camp at Cirencester. We arrived by coach on some big country estate surrounded by a stone wall, with guards at the entrance gate. It felt like being locked in prison together with five other boys and I slept next to a senior NCO, Dick Kelsey. He was a Sergeant, who came each year and knew all the 'ins and outs'. We had an awful meal before lights-out , suet pudding and the most horrible custard I have ever tasted. I ended up washing my plate and cutlery in a bucket that had more suet and custard than water so I had to walk miles to a tap to wash them. The next day we were up at first light to parade. Some holiday! Lunch was stew and more suet and custard and then quickly to the wash pail. Every day was the same old routine, drilling, route march, suet, custard and stew. All I was looking forward to was going to bed. And then came the final day; at last. We were up at dawn and cleared the whole area, pulled down the tents and folded them up, leaving everything in neat rows, then marched to the carriage. Finally, we were on the bus and I was determined to make my parents life hell when I got back but I soon forgot all about that at the joy of being home to roast lamb with mint sauce. During my one week stay I learned that if you get on with your seniors, all the rotten tasks are given to other people. Mostly I learned to appreciate good food and a comfortable bed.

I remember one particular Christmas, I was about 13, had just won my Surrey Marksman's badge at school and was trying to talk my father into buying me an airgun for Christmas. Lo and behold, Christmas morning there by the side of my bed was a Diana Airgun. Oh boy! It cost 12s 6d as I remember, which was quite a lot of money in those days, plus two packets of slugs, with about 200 slugs in each. Well, what a day I had! We had two apple trees at the end of the garden, Beauty of Bath, full of apples (lovely). I sat at the upstairs window of my bedroom with my gun after breakfast, and started shooting at these apples. I thought to myself: *either I'm not as good a shot as I think I am, or there's something wrong with the sights of the gun*. After I had fired about 100 pellets and knocked only one apple down. I went downstairs, and to the back of the garden to have a look at the apple tree and what a mess I had made. Each little pellet had gone in one side of an apple, come straight out the other side and taken half the apple with it leaving the rest of the apple hanging on the tree. Most of the apples on the tree were a shambles, so I went smartly back into my bedroom, saying nothing and hoping I would not be found out. During the evening, I saw George and Tom Thomas opposite, getting ready going out to a dance, so I fired a pellet at their window just to give it a bit of a tap, but unfortunately it broke the window and just missed them. The next thing their father was at the front door. Well, that was the end of it. My old man took the gun away, I lost my pocket money for two weeks to pay for the window, and on Monday morning he took the gun back to Gamages, less the pellets because I had used almost all the slugs, firing at anything I could find!

Chapter 3

Working life

By the time I was 14 years old, it was obvious that I would never be an academic so my parents decided I'd be better off with a job. My father had met somebody in a caravan park while on holiday, who was manager of a stockbroking office in London, who said he would give me a job as an office boy, so I started work after the summer holiday in September in 1935. Not having a suit, I went up to London in my Tiffinian blazer which was royal blue with vertical red stripes. It was very, very bright. Everybody seemed to look at me and I felt most self conscious. Fortunately, later that week my father took me to the Fifty Shilling Tailors in Kingston-on-Thames where I bought my first suit which actually cost fifty shillings! A nice grey pin-striped suit – and very proud of it I was too.

I worked for the stockbrokers Blount & Company for eighteen months. I started off at fifteen shillings a week which went up to 17s 6d a week. That was enough to buy me sandwiches every day, pay for a weekly rail ticket, pay five shillings housekeeping to my mother and still left me with change at the end of the week to go to the pictures. I also remember buying my first shares, a thousand Anglo-Java Rubber at a halfpenny, and selling them for a penny ha'penny, which was a great joke in the office. Although I did not realise it at the time, I was running around London carrying thousands of dollars' worth of bearer bonds, like United States Steel and International Nickel and they were all Bearer Bonds! God when I think of it, the trust that these people put on you. I could have easily lost them or 'done' something with them.

I had that job for eighteen months but wasn't getting anywhere, so I got a job with a tobacco merchant. A Jewish man called Soloman in Leggnore Street – a bit further towards the East End of London. He had lots of tobacco leaf, which he used to sell to tobacco merchants, as well as making his own cigarettes on a hand machine. I would get there half an hour earlier than anybody else to open up and get the place ready and in which time I would put some leaf through the machine to make my own cigarettes. I lived on free cigarettes and supplied my friends while I was there. Sadly, that job only lasted six weeks because my father thought I should go into a profession and got me a job with *Sayers*, an Incorporated Accountant just round the corner from home. He paid my articles (£100), and I was set to do all the examinations to become an accountant.

At that, time the Royal Air Force were giving a lot of four year, and six year Short Service Commissions because they could see a war was coming in the near future and needed pilots. Unfortunately, you had to be of matriculation standard and, because I'd left school at 14 years old, I did not have my General School Certificate let alone matriculation. One of my neighbours – a scholarship boy at Surbiton County – had no problem at all with matriculation. He was already in training, so I decided that I would give it a go anyway. I completed all the necessary form claiming that I had reached matriculation standard. My father needed to sign them but my mother put her foot down because she didn't want me going into the Air Force 'to get killed', so my father refused to sign them. Determined not to be stopped, I pulled out my pen and, upside down like I had learnt at school, forged my father's signature and sent it off to the Air Ministry. Our postman used to come early in the morning so I would rush downstairs ahead of my parents to see if there was a letter for me. After a few weeks, the hoped-for letter arrived. I was to report to the Air Ministry at nine o'clock one morning during the week for an interview, with a medical test and a psychology test to follow. Naturally, I said nothing to my parents and, when the day came, I called *Sayers* and told them I was sick and while my parents thought I was at work, off I went on the train from Surbiton to the Air Ministry at Holborn. When the time came for my interview, I was shown into a room where three venerable old gentlemen were sitting at a long table. I sat down in front of them while they looked me over, and asked me some questions. I can still remember what they were: "What are lines of latitude and longitude?" Which I could answer, because I liked my geography so I had no problem. "Which were longer; and why?" Which I answered all right. However the last question was: "What is a Rhombus?" I wasn't too good at geometry so, thinking on my feet, I told them that Rhombus invaded England with Remus. Fortunately, that seemed to amuse them because I saw smiles on a couple of faces and the next thing I knew, I was through. I had a medical and psychology test after the interview and got home at my usual time so my parents still didn't catch on.

Then I waited and waited until finally, one morning, it came: YOU HAVE BEEN ACCEPTED ON A SHORT SERVICE COMMISSION and will report to No.11 E & RFTS, Perth. Scotland on the 2nd of February.

That was 1939. I told my parents the whole story, including how I had forged Dad's signature. There were eruptions, there was a lot of 'what they were going to do' and 'how they were going to tell' and what trouble I was in, but in the end they had to accept it and that was that. My father did ask what I intended to do about the £100 he had paid for Articles; I told him I would pay him back as soon as I had earned the money and we left it at that.

Chapter 4

Training. No.2 FTS, Brize Norton

May 1939

Mum and Dad saw me off a few weeks later at Kings Cross Station on the train up to Perth. From Perth, I was taken by bus to Scone Airport where I was shown to a little bungalow before meeting all the other fellows who were starting the course. Most of whom were public school boys and had attended either Eton or Harrow. There were a few like me and I quickly teamed up with a fellow named Brownlow and a Canadian by the name of Cameron. The first day I was there, I was given the name "Percy" because I was a real innocent which stuck with me until I left the Air Force eight and a half years later. Even now people write to me from England, "Dear Percy". We remained in Perth until April 1939 and learned to fly Tiger Moths.

I went solo in about eight and half hours, nothing exceptional and longer than most people, but once I was solo I was alright and really enjoyed the fun of flying. I also had my first sexual experience, as it were. We went into Perth on a Saturday night to a big dance where I met a girl and danced, although I could not dance to save my life. At the end of the evening she asked me to walk her home and of course I said I would. Part way home, she led me into an alleyway, kissed me with her mouth open and put her hands between my legs. I was terrified and ended up running all three miles back to the Airport!

I once ran into trouble with the Armament Instructor over a Vickers machine-gun which was, at that time, the number one gun in the RAF. We had to dissemble it and put it together within a certain time. Every now and then he would refer to a certain part as 'the gubbins' and, like an idiot, I stood up in front of the class and said: "Could you please tell me what 'the gubbins' is – I haven't found it yet". He thought I was being smart with him and after that I never really got on with him, he used to do all sorts of rotten things to get at me. The first time I ever did an inverted spin in a Tiger Moth was also the last. Towards the end of the course my instructor thought I was ready to give it a try so we got to a good height and turned on our backs (flying upside-down). Then he announced his intention to do an inverted spin and he pulled the nose of the aircraft up, upside-down and put on full rudder, so that we began to spin. With an inverted spin, you are on the outside of the spin and the centrifugal force tries to throw you out of the aircraft. Well, it was the most awful feeling. I couldn't even get my feet on to the rudders, I was hanging by the straps on the outside of this spin while centrifugal force was trying to throw me out. I realised that if I ever got into one of these spins on my own, I'd never get out again because I couldn't reach the rudders. My Instructor enjoyed my discomfort very much; he thought that was great and had a good laugh at my expense.

At the end of our course we had a big party and I got nicely pie-eyed, I had only just started drinking so it didn't take much. Next day we all travelled by train down to Uxbridge, where we spent most of our time going into London, being fitted out with our uniforms then taking the rest of the day off. From there we were all posted to No.2 FTS at Brize Norton near Whitney in Oxfordshire. None of us knew what we would be flying at Brize Norton, but most of us hoped that we would be on single engined aircraft because that would lead us onto fighters. Two thirds of the course, myself included, went onto Airspeed Oxfords, which were the twin engined training aircrafts, and the other third went onto Harvards, which were North American single engine training aircraft. Most people who went on to the Harvards thought they would move on to fighters but things didn't turn out quite as they hoped. In the end, the choice of training aircraft seemed to have no influence over which plane you would go on to fly. I was very fortunate in the end because I was assigned to a fighter, I was far happier in a single engined aircraft and could see myself shooting down enemy aircraft right, left and centre. From May until November 1939, we did our Senior FTS course. They were great days; I look back on them now and probably think them greater than they really were. Brize Norton was a lovely spot, three miles from Whitney and a mile from a pub where we used to go at night, right on the banks of the River Thames, which was only about 25 yds wide at that spot. The beautiful city of Oxford was only about 15 miles away. I thoroughly enjoyed the six months I spent at Brize Norton – though I did get into a certain amount of bother, as was my want. This did not change throughout my Air Force career.

I went solo in an Airspeed Oxford after two or three hours and did all the exercises I was supposed to do. The first navigational exercise was a different story however. I went and got lost. I knew I was in the right vicinity but couldn't see anything that I recognised and was getting low on fuel, so when I saw a large airfield below me I went into land. As I came into land I was greeted by a lot of red lights fired at me from Very pistols. I ignored them because I did not think they were for me until I came in and landed right in front of three Fairey Battle light bombers taking off in formation. Fortunately, they missed me, but when I had taxied in I was marched straight to the Chief Flying Instructor, and given an awful 'rocket' which I remember to this day. He even phoned up the CFO in Brize Norton and told him what had happened.

I had landed at Abingdon – only about 10 miles from where I was stationed. My Oxford was re-fuelled and I took off for home. When I landed back at Brize, I was immediately summoned before the Chief Flying Instructor who gave me another 'rocket' and made me Duty Officer for three days which meant I couldn't leave the base .

There were Prefects on our course to keep us in some sort of order, as it were and one was an awful bastard by the name of Ralston. Angus Cameron and myself didn't like Ralston, so we went into his room one day, filled his socks with jelly and put marbles under the under sheets of his bed. He soon found out who was responsible and reported us both to the Chief Ground Instructor. Consequently, Angus Cameron and myself were confined to camp and missed out on a three day long weekend. Everybody went off for the weekend and the Station was practically empty except for us two and even then we managed to get into trouble because we went onto the grass airfield with a golf stick and some balls. We were hitting them around and sent one flying straight through the Tower window, which did not make us very popular.

During the first month of our training, we were given a squad of twenty to thirty airmen and had to drill them; march them backwards and forwards, form fours, form twos, and slope arms etc, etc. I was absolutely hopeless a drilling a squad, I could never get the right foot. In fact, once when I had them marching, I marched them straight off the Parade Ground, over the road and into the Barrack Block before I called them to a halt! Once again I was made to come back early from a long weekend and had to spend it on the Parade Ground drilling airmen. In October the whole course was sent to Armament Camp at Porthcawl in South Wales. Angus Cameron, Brownlow and myself were all great mates at Perth and still the greatest friends throughout Brize Norton. When we left

Brize Norton for Porthcawl at the end of our course though, we never saw each other again. Angus Cameron went to do a course on Navigation, because he was going on Coastal Command, within a month he had gone out to sea on an exercise and was never seen again. Brownlow went onto a Whitley Squadron of heavy Bombers and I don't know what happened to him, or whether he got through the War.

For those of us flying the Airspeed Oxfords, our time in Porthcawl consisted of flying and firing a Vickers K gun from a turret, at Drogue targets towed by Henley Aircraft. Also dropping 12 lb practice bombs on a target about two to three miles out to sea. The Armament Camp itself was a 'danger area' and the public were not allowed to go near it. We arrived there by air and all the ground crews came by train and road. When we got there we found that we had been allotted the Beach Hotel, the best hotel in Porthcawl, we spent a month there and had a thoroughly enjoyable time because we didn't have to go far to drink, and consequently we drank quite a lot. One of my best friends there was a little Canadian by the name of 'Smiley' Robinson, he was the funniest little man I had ever met in my life. Poor old Smiley went to 235 Squadron, a newly formed squadron of Bristol Blenheim bombers, and within twelve months he was shot down and killed by one of our own aircraft.

One night four of us got a bit drunk and went out to the garden in the Hotel's courtyard, which had a white limestone statue of a little boy with curly hair and a pan. Using Indian Ink we gave him spectacles and a moustache, as well as painting his private parts – which was hilarious at the time. The manager didn't think it was funny the next morning. He called the CO, who had us on parade to find out who did it and we all owned, so we spent the whole of the next day with buckets, scrubbing brushes and soap getting the black ink off which had sunk into the white limestone. It took us all day to get it off but even then there were still faint marks.

At the beginning of November we returned to Brize Norton where we passed out of the course and were presented with our Wings. The next day we were given our postings and I was posted to 253 Squadron at Manston in Kent along with about twenty others from the course. We thought that was great since Manston was one of the plum Fighter stations in the Air Force. However we were told we were going onto Blenheims, which didn't please us very much because they had very little defence and took an awful pounding in the war.

Chapter 5

253 Squadron. RAF Manston

November 1939

We travelled to Margate, which was near Manston, by train on 6 November. It was a dark dreary night and there was nobody at Margate Station to meet us, so we 'phoned Manston and then went to the nearest pub for an hour until a van picked us up. When we finally arrived, we were showed our billets and had a couple of drinks in the Mess before going to bed. The next day I found I had been assigned to 'A' Flight, with Flight Lieutenant Anderson, a Canadian, as my Flight Commander. The other Flight Commander, in 'B' Flight, was a fellow named Guy Harris, who had come from 32 Squadron, also a Flight Lieutenant. It transpired that we were not going to be flying twin engine bombers after all, but were forming a new single engine fighter squadron. The Air Force had decided that they were so short of single-engined fighter squadrons that they were going to form four new Squadrons. Thinking we would be flying Hawker Hurricanes, we were delighted with the news, but when we went to see all these lovely Hurricanes, we found out that we only had two Miles Magister training aircraft. The whole squadron was there, all the men, all the pilots, CO, Flight Commanders – everybody was there, but we had nothing to fly but the two Magisters which were small monoplanes similar in size and cockpit layout to a Tiger Moth.

We flew these around for a few weeks or so and I can remember going up with Joe Hobbs one day and 'shooting up' his father who was a real estate auctioneer who lived at Ashford nearby. About three weeks later we were equipped with, of all things, Fairey Battles. We were all thoroughly disappointed but were told not to worry, we'd only have the Fairey Battles for a couple of months, and then we would be re-equipped with Hurricanes. That made our day, so we didn't really mind. We had a cockpit drill, then took off, and found that the Fairey Battle was a really a nice aeroplane to fly. It had few vices but a very comfortable cockpit and joystick to hold, we quite enjoyed flying around the country in them. I did get caught in a fog one day. I took off from Manston, did a cross country somewhere and as I came back, fog had rolled in from the sea meaning I couldn't land at Manston because the fog had come right in over the aerodrome. I had flown straight into the bank of fog, so I turned round using my instruments – the first real instrument flying in cloud I had done. My artificial horizon was showing an angle of about forty or fifty degrees, which I found very hard to believe because it meant I was in a turn when I felt certain I was straight and level. I did believe it eventually though because I realised that I was getting steeper into the turn and knew I had to correct it, against my better instincts, because if I didn't do it immediately I was going to kill myself. Soon I was flying out of cloud at a few thousand feet on top of a high bank of fog. I flew inland in clear sky to land at Redhill and spent the night there, returning to Manston the next morning having learned one essential lesson: Believe Your Instruments!

One of the few cars at Manston was a canvas-hooded Austin 7 of 1927 vintage owned by a fellow named Curly Clifton. One morning I came down to breakfast to find a really comical sight; there was Curly's Austin, perpendicular and normal up to the main body, but the canvas top and frame were bent at an angle of forty-five degrees. Soon a few very hung-over bodies arrived late for breakfast, Curly amongst them and we finally got the story. Curly "Jenks" Jenkins, "Joe" Hobbs and Peter Dawbarn had piled into the car for a session in Margate. On the return journey, all very 'happy', they came upon a roundabout and someone bet that the car could not go round at full speed; needless to say they did try but came to grief and the car turned over on its back. They all clambered out uninjured, set the car onto its four wheels again and drove back to Manston. All arrived safely and, except for the framework of the car, in sterling order. After breakfast, between all of us and the help of crowbars and hammers, it soon looked as good as new.

In February we were re-equipped with the Hurricane Mark I. They weren't new mind you, we got two aircraft from each Hurricane Squadron, so you can imagine what condition the aircraft were in. We got the two worst Hurricanes from each Squadron, fixed pitched props, no mirrors, no armour plating. That's how 253 Squadron was formed, but we couldn't have cared less – it was wonderful that we were about to fly a real fighter. After having a cockpit drill and a little test, I took off for the first time on 10 February 1940 for experience, a total of two landings and take-offs according to my Log Book. Later in the month, we had to deliver our Fairey Battles to Silloth on the Solway Firth in Cumberland and I was one of the pilots involved. I took off on a straight trip with no landings in between to refuel and all went well until I got to Doncaster, where the visibility had closed in to about 2,000 yards. It was a rotten day for seeing anything down below, so I followed the railway line from Doncaster, which has about eight lines going out from it. Unfortunately I took the wrong line and instead of getting to Silloth, I finished up landing at Squires Gate in Blackpool – where I had a very good night! The next day I flew up from there to Silloth which was only a twenty minute journey.

In mid-February, the whole of the squadron was posted to Northolt which we all thought was great because Northolt was a northern suburb of London and was on the Underground, making it very simple to get into London each night if we wanted to. Northolt was an old type station so we had comfortable quarters, 65 Squadron Spitfires were also based there. Their Flight Commander was an Australian by the name of Gordon Olive who I got to know much better after the war when I moved to Australia. They also had the best pilot in the RAF – Flying Officer Stanford-Tuck. The two squadrons got on very well and had lots of fun together. Meanwhile, we were gaining experience on our Hurricanes, doing navigational exercises to get used to flying in single-engined fast aircraft without getting lost. We also practised air to ground firing on Dengie Flats, which is marsh land off Essex. This was great fun, firing eight machine guns at targets in the marsh; we thought this was wonderful. During our free time we used to go into London at night; so the boys decided that "Percy" (the name I had been given as I was still a virgin) was going to lose his virginity. I was 18-years-old and very nervous of the opposite sex. I would not, in my wildest dreams, have asked a girl to sleep with me, unless, of course, under the influence of alcohol which was still a novelty to me.

In March 1940, some of my mates took me to my first night club: The Bag of Nails somewhere in the West End of London. We paid a sum of money to enter and went downstairs into a dim, smoke-filled large room where a band was playing and there were as many women as men. We were shown to a table and ordered drinks. The hostesses were what we would now call high-class call-girls, though I did not know that at the time, of course. After a few brandies I danced with a lovely little blonde girl in a slinky, low-cut dress. She pressed her pelvis into my body with great effect and I embarrassingly acquired an erection, which I hoped she would think was something in my pocket – that's how innocent I was! However, she soon made it clear that she wanted me to go home with her and sleep the night. I couldn't believe my luck, until we got back to our table where she then told me that it would be five pounds! At that time, as a Pilot Officer, I was earning 12s 6d a day so it was more than a week's wages. Unfortunately, I was so drunk that she seemed the loveliest woman I had ever met and the money didn't matter. Without further ado, I wrote a cheque for the sum required and we said farewell to my mates who, I found out afterwards, had set the whole thing up. They knew the girl and had told her that I was still a virgin. We got into a taxi and she gave her address and started a very heavy snogging session while her hands were doing most unbelievable things! The next thing I remember was waking up in a single bed on my own. I couldn't remember a thing after getting into the taxi and didn't know what had happened or where I was. My lady-friend of the previous night must have heard my stirrings because she entered the bedroom, asked how I felt and said I had better get dressed and back to Northolt or I would be late. Even at that hour, without make-up, she was still attractive and I was too embarrassed to ask whether I had lost my virginity or not.

I arrived back at Northolt at 11 am and was immediately asked to report to the CO. The adjutant marched me in where I received an imperial rocket for not being at readiness at 8 am. I was also told that I smelled like a brewery and that, as from the next day, I would be Squadron Orderly Officer for a week. I was reminded of my escapade for the next few days by the occasional whiff of the most seductive perfume on my uniform. Two days later my bank called to ask whether it was in order to pay a cheque for five pounds because my signature could not be recognised. As a gentleman, I honoured the cheque and told them to pay it; but asked if they could send the cheque itself to me by post. It arrived the following day and became the joke of the Mess for a while because it appeared to have been written by a 6-year-old and was practically illegible.

Another night we went up to London didn't end quite so well. We were all in a club, drinking brandy – which I was still not used to and had drunk far too much. A lovely young woman was doing the dance of the Seven Veils near our table and, to my shame, I ended up being sick under the table while she danced for my mates. I remember very little after we left the club and was horrified to wake up the next morning in a prison cell. I couldn't believe my eyes! I had a terrible hangover and was in a cell with bars on the door. I got out of the bunk I was sleeping on, rattled on the door and shouted. A policeman came to the cell door, looked in and said, "Ah, you have come to." He opened the door and let me out. When I asked what I had done to deserve being locked up, he told me I hadn't done anything, but had been discovered lying on the pavement just off Shaftesbury Avenue. Apparently, I was so unconscious that they couldn't revive me so they put me on a stretcher and brought me to the police station for safe-keeping. I was a Pilot Officer in full uniform cap, greatcoat, the lot. The police thought it was a great joke and I finished up in their canteen having a fried breakfast, even with a hangover.

Our two months at Northolt went quickly. Our days were spent getting used to the Hurricane, slinging it around the sky, doing aerobatics which I had never done flying on 'Oxfords'. So I had to learn aerobatics on my own as the only aerobatics I had done was on Tiger Moths! Most of our nights were spent on the town either in London or in the local pubs. Then, on 9 May, we were posted to Kenley, which was also an old type of station, on a hill near Purley, just south of Croydon. Not long after my nineteenth birthday, a few of us went into London and ended up at The Paradise Club.

We staggered out of the club in the early hours of the morning, inebriated but happy and with a girl or two in our midst. The girl I had paired up with asked me to take her to a hotel for the night. As luck would have it, the girlfriend of my mate Joe Hobbs was also the receptionist at the South Kensington Hotel, which made it simple for us to get a room at two in the morning. Although I was drunk, I was nowhere near as paralytic as I had been the last time I'd spent the night with a woman and was determined to enjoy the experience. Unfortunately, I was so nervous that the whole thing was over before it had even begun.

I woke up in the early hours and slid stealthily out of bed, dressed and sneaked out of the room. I caught first the tube and then a bus back to Kenley. I thought that was the end of the story, but I was wrong. Joe received a 'phone call later that morning from his partner of the previous night, who was the receptionist at the hotel. She was 'phoning on behalf of the girl I had slept with, to inform me that our room had not been paid for and that the lady concerned had no money and would I kindly settle up. It was a complete oversight on my part, but I had every intention of paying and sent the money to Joe's girl who settled up for me.

Shortly after this episode the war began in earnest. The Germans invaded Holland and Belgium and Joe was posted to another squadron and I never saw him again. He was killed over El Adem in North Africa in 1941.

Chapter 6

The Battle of France, Lille Marque

Excerpt from Winston Churchill's First Broadcast as Prime Minister. Aired by the BBC on May 19, 1940.

In the air – often at serious odds, often at odds hitherto thought overwhelming – we have been clawing down three or four to one of our enemies; and the relative balance of the British and German Air Forces is now considerably more favourable to us than at the beginning of the battle. In cutting down the German bombers, we are fighting our own battle as well as that of France. My confidence in our ability to fight it out to the finish with the German Air Force has been strengthened by the fierce encounters which have taken place and are taking place.

May 1940

On 15 May 1940, our squadron was warned that we were going over to France to fight, but not as a whole squadron. We were being split up with one flight going to Lille and the other going to Vitry while the CO and Adjutant remained in England. I was in 'A' Flight which was going to Vitry but in the end, 'B' Flight was short so I was sent to Lille. We were warned on the fifteenth that an Armstrong Whitworth Ensign was coming to pick up our ground troops, all their kit and our kit, we were to take everything, leave nothing behind, and load it all onto this large four engined Ensign aircraft which would transport it to Lille for us. I put my golf clubs, my electric razor and everything that I possessed onto this. On the sixteenth, 'B' Flight consisting of Flight Lieutenant Anderson and Pilot Officers Clifton, Jenkins, Dawbarn, McKenzie and myself, were sent to Lille at an hour's notice. Our flight left for Manston, where we stayed the night then on the seventeenth we took off in the morning, following a Bristol Blenheim which took us to Lille Marque. This was a very large fallow field, no hangers on it, just an open field with Hurricanes spread all the way around it. We landed there and taxied up to one end of the field, and there we stayed until an air-raid siren sounded in Lille At the sound of the air-raid siren, all serviceable aircraft took off because it meant that enemy aircraft were in the vicinity.

The squadrons were spread all over the field. Everybody took off in all directions from all over the field. We were on our own but soon tagged up with all the other aircraft that had taken off. How we missed each other I don't know – there simply was no organisation whatsoever. We still had the same old Hurricanes, with wooden fixed props, no armour and no rear view mirrors; we were the only aircraft on the field like that. We tried to join forces with 504 Squadron but the CO, Squadron Leader Rook, wouldn't have anything to do with us. Our radios were old TR9D sets, which gave us a range of about two miles with lots of static and were absolutely useless. We joined up with other aircraft of unknown squadrons and tried to follow them. We managed to avoid the enemy and find our way safely back to the airfield. My Log Book shows that we did a patrol of Douax and Cambrai at 20,000 ft and encountered nothing.

There was no accommodation for us that first night so we had to sleep in a tent, lying on stretchers in our flying gear with only a blanket to protect us from the freezing cold. We got barely any sleep at all and were up early the next morning. I was standing in the early mist and cold when I saw two Lysanders, Army Co-op machines, making their final approach to land. Suddenly, four Me109's came out of nowhere and attacked the Lysanders from behind. I don't remember hearing any sound whatsoever, just the Me109's flying away and both Lysanders diving straight into the ground and going up in a huge burst of flame. I suppose I can't remember any sound, because I was in a state of shock. That was my initiation into air warfare and I realised it was deadly serious.

For breakfast we walked to a little café at the edge of the airfield, where we had coffee and rolls. Later that morning the sirens sounded, and off we went; all taking off in a great Balbo or large formation. It was all a bit of a shambles because we didn't know where we were going. We got up to 15-16,000 ft and ran into a big group of thirty or forty Dorniers and Messerschmitt 110s. I had forgotten to put my sights on and by the time I had got my sights onto an aircraft and pressed the button, I found that my guns were on safe and had to turn them on. By this time I was in the midst of dozens of German aircraft, but I got behind one and gave him a great 'burst', a Dornier which I believe was shot down. I became separated from the others and found myself alone and lost, so I went down onto the first airfield I saw with aircraft on it, which turned out to be Merville – I was completely lost. I was refuelled and then returned to Lille to find out that Jenkins had been shot down and his aircraft was a 'write-off'. Fortunately, he was alright and managed to get a lift back. A lot of our aircraft had been badly damaged and we only had about four fit for flying.

The following day all our aircraft were supposed to take off and rendezvous with some Fairey Battles and escort them to Cambrai. We climbed to 15,000 ft which seemed to be the fighting height in those days, but found no Luftwaffe. Then, we were suddenly engaged by

German aircraft and became separated. I was on my own trying to find out where I was, when suddenly an Me109, all on its own, passed just below me about 100 ft down. This time I had my sights and guns ON – I had learnt to put them on before I took off, otherwise I'd forget. I dived after the Messerschmitt, came up behind it and gave it a long burst of fire. Our guns were loaded with de Wilde ammunition, which gave off a white puff of smoke, rather like tracer, only more accurate. It shook me because it looked just as if the German aircraft was firing at me. I could see eight streams of bullets coming straight back at my wings. It scared the daylights out of me until I realised that it was me firing into the German aircraft! I continued to fire until my guns were empty and the 109 continued straight down into the ground. The pilot did not get out of it and that was my second 'kill'. There was a huge cloud of black, grey smoke and orange flame. I was only 19 years of age and remember feeling elated while I was firing at him; but not when he hit the ground. It shook me considerably, as it so easily could have been me. I learned then to never stop looking around and above, which held me in good stead later on.

When I found my way back to Lille I discovered that Flight Commander Anderson had not returned and another pilot, Sergeant McKenzie was also missing. Eventually we found out that both had been killed. We were told to evacuate as the Germans had just about cut us off. On the evening of the 19 May, the remains of 'B' Flight flew back to Kenley. We had been away barely three days but most of our aircraft were shot-up and unserviceable and we had lost two pilots. When we flew back there were only three of us with serviceable aircraft; the other Hurricanes were broken up with axes. The squadron personnel took to the lorries and came back to England via Boulogne, dumping all our worldly goods, including my golf clubs I might add, into Boulogne Harbour. So when we got back, we had nothing but the clothes we stood up in. We were given £25 to re-equip ourselves which was totally inadequate, so we spent some time flying to various airfields and scrounging other people's kit. In other words: stealing it off the pegs!

We weren't the only squadron to suffer losses in France. When we got back we found that 'A' Flight at Vitry had also suffered. Their Flight Commander, Guy Harris, was in hospital and three other pilots had been killed or wounded. Meanwhile, I found out that my parents had 'phoned the station and had been told that I was missing, so they were in a fair old tizzy. I was given a day off to go back and see them.

After that we started flying Channel Patrol to Boulogne and Dunkirk, where we could see the oil storage tanks burning. Having lost both our flight commanders in France, our CO, Squadron Leader Elliott, had to lead us and, on 20 May, what was left of the squadron escorted twenty-four Blenheims to bomb Arras. We met no opposition on this occasion and all of us returned intact to Kenley. On 21 May, we patrolled Arras to Cambrai and were weaving amongst the Ack Ack when suddenly there was no CO. I did not see him disappear and there were no enemy fighters around. So now we were a squadron with neither CO nor Flight Commanders. Squadron Leader Elliott was posted as missing and I found out after the war that he had been a prisoner of war (POW) and had not been shot down, but landed purposely behind enemy lines because he did not want to fight in the War.[1] We made several of these trips over to France to escort Ensigns and Douglas DC3s to Merville and, on

---

1. The loss of Squadron Leader Elliott has differing accounts. What is known is that he enjoyed a long post-war RAF career and retired in 1955 with the rank of Group Captain.

23 May, to escort and bring out other squadrons, troops and people who were surrounded by the enemy and we got into a great big dog-fight over Merville. I shot down an Me109 which attacked one of our Hurricanes above me and then dived vertically for the ground, straight through my gun sight. I gave him a good burst, which must have gone through the top of his roof! He went quickly, I did not see what happened to him but 'Curly' Clifton saw him carry on straight down and he did not pull out so I claimed it as a victory.

I came back on my own and it was very, misty over the Channel with visibility down to 2,000 yds, so I flew due West thinking that I must hit England somewhere, then I could re-orientate myself. After I had flown for half an hour I could still see no land whatsoever. I thought, as I had very little fuel left, I might be flying down the Thames estuary, but after another ten or fifteen minutes I had already turned onto my reserve tanks. I thought if I was North, I would have hit the land by now; but if I was South, I would still be going out parallel along the South Coast and at sea. Visibility was still only about 2,000 yards, so I immediately turned North and within two minutes I had hit the coast, seen an aerodrome down below me and landed. It turned out to be Ford Aerodrome which was a Royal Naval Air station and as I landed and taxied in, my engine cut out. I had completely run out of fuel. They pulled me in by tractor, then I went to the Mess and told all these naval fellows that had gathered around me the story about the big fight we had had 'over there '. They were all very jealous of me and gave me lots of pink gin. I returned to Kenley after lunch under the 'allfluence of Inkahole', but pleased to be alive. The next day, 24 May, the squadron moved from Kenley to Kirton-in-Lindsey to re-form, we also received a new CO and two Flight Commanders, together with some new pilots straight from OTU and only a few hours on Hurricanes.

In retrospect, the Battle of France could only be described a disorganised shambles; no leadership, no food and half the squadron lost in a week. That week seemed the longest week of my life. We had been told that the German aircraft were inferior to our Hurricanes, however we soon found out that the Me109 was superior in terms of armament, speed, dive, climb and maximum height. We also discovered that the Me110 was not an aircraft to attack head-on, because its armament was superior, otherwise the Hurricane outclassed it. Far too many Hurricanes were lost and what is more we lost some very good pilots over France who would have been a great help in the Battle of Britain; but those of us who survived learned a lot about the German aircraft and pilots. In the three days we spent at Lille Marque, I learned enough to emerge alive from the Battle of Britain later on.

Chapter 7

The Squadron Reforms,
RAF Kirton-in-Lindsey

Excerpt from Winston Churchill's speech, House of Commons, 4 June 1940.

May it not also be that the cause of civilization itself will be defended by the skill and devotion of a few thousand airmen? There never has been, I suppose, in all the world, in all the history of war, such an opportunity for youth. The Knights of the Round Table, the Crusaders, all fall back into the past-not only distant but prosaic; these young men, going forth every morn to guard their native land and all that we stand for, holding in their hands these instruments of colossal and shattering power, of whom it may be said that

> Every morn brought forth a noble chance.
> And every chance brought forth a noble knight,

deserve our gratitude, as do all the brave men who, in so many ways and on so many occasions, are ready, and continue ready to give life and all for their native land.

June 1940

We landed at Kirton-in-Lindsey on 24 May and were met by a station wagon that collected the pilots and took us to the mess, which was about two miles away. One by one we were picked up by this gentleman who limped and appeared to have a gammy leg. Later we found out he was Douglas Bader who was then a Flight Commander on 222 Squadron, Spitfires, which was already at Kirton-in-Lindsey. When we arrived, we found that we had a new CO by the name of Atcherly, or 'Batchey' Atcherly as he was commonly known. He was one of the famous Atcherly brothers, notorious throughout the Royal Air Force for doing all sorts of odd things. They were very good pilots, but completely mad. We had two new Flight Commanders, Flight Lieutenant George Brown and Flight Lieutenant Bill Cambridge, who was shot down and killed not long after the start of the Battle of Britain. A few new pilots joined us too, including Carthew and Francis who, because they were teamed up together, were known as 'Tweedle Dum and Tweedle Dee'. My great friend there was a New Zealander, Jack Strang, who was a good rugby player and had been in the squadron a little while. He had been in 'A' Flight at Vitry in France, and had got out scot-free.

Kirton-in-Lindsey station was still being completed and we had no transport from dispersal to the Officers Mess about half a mile away. It was here that Curly's car was to come once again to our rescue. Unfortunately, the Austin 7 was not registered so was without petrol coupons. What we did was buy a quantity of little sausage-like gelatine refills for petrol cigarette lighters, fill the carburettor up to the top and pile onto the car, sometimes seven or eight of us, both inside and outside the car. It must have been quite a sight, but was probably safer for all concerned when this stopped and we were finally given official transport.

We had only been there for a day when 'Batchy' Atcherly was already on the 'phone to the Air Ministry. He was onto the Air Ministry every day to say that our squadron was simply leaping in its seats to get down there and over Dunkirk to shoot some Germans down. When in actual fact, we were all still shaken by our experiences in France and just wanted to rest. We didn't care if we didn't see another German aircraft for months! We were completely demoralised, a situation made worse by the fact that we were being brought up to strength with new pilots having only a few hours flying experience on Hurricanes.

'Batchy' was such a bloody nuisance to the Air Ministry that within five days he was posted up to Wick, which was about as far north as you could go in Scotland. Even there he got into trouble. Apparently he took off in a Magister, spotted an aircraft carrier not too far from Scapa Flow, a large Royal Navy Base in the Orkneys, and against all the signals, he landed on the deck. Unfortunately the lift was down and he went straight down one of the lifts that brought the planes up from below! I don't know what happened after that, I was just glad that he left our squadron. His replacement was Squadron Leader Tom Gleave, who became well known throughout the UK as President of the Guinea Pig Club. Tom was a great bloke; you couldn't hope to meet a nicer man. While we were in Kirton-in-Lindsey we were re-equipped with newer Hurricanes that had constant speed props, armour plating and mirrors. They were absolutely magnificent after our old wrecks. We really began to enjoy flying again.

In July we were moved to Turnhouse, near Edinburgh and were joined by Squadron Leader King who took over as Squadron Commander with Squadron Leader Gleave being made a

Supernumerary Squadron Leader. We did not understand why this was done; but the reasons were clear enough once the Battle started and we began losing leaders. King was only with us for about four weeks but that was enough. He was, in my opinion, a nut-case. He was killed later in the Battle of Britain while in another squadron. Our next Squadron Leader after that was a man called Harold Starr.

We were all keen to return south because it was August and we were hearing and reading all about the Battle of Britain. How the enemy were losing hundreds of aircraft while we were only losing one or two! All we could think of was shooting down enemy aircraft again. We thought this would be far better than when we were in France, it had to be. Then on the night of 28 August, while we were all at the Blossoms Hotel near Prestwick, having a few beers and getting nicely happy, we got a 'phone call from Tom Gleave at Prestwick station. He had just arrived back from leave and had been told that we were off the next day, posted down to Kenley to take part in the 'Battle''. We all left the pub, got back to the Mess, invited all the Sergeant Pilots around and had great wrestling matches. I went three rounds with Bill Cambridge – I won one and he won the last two. We also had a game of rugby with cushions and the Mess ended up completely covered with feathers. Then we all retired to bed and got up the next morning a little bit hazy, but all ready to go.

Excerpt from Winston Churchill's speech, House of Commons, 18 June 1940.

What General Weygand called the Battle of France is over. I expect that the Battle of Britain is about to begin. Upon this battle depends the survival of Christian civilization. Upon it depends our own British life, and the long continuity of our institutions and our Empire. The whole fury and might of the enemy must very soon be turned on us. Hitler knows that he will have to break us in this Island or lose the war. If we can stand up to him, all Europe may be free and the life of the world may move forward into broad, sunlit uplands. But if we fail, then the whole world, including the United States, including all that we have known and cared for, will sink into the abyss of a new Dark Age made more sinister, and perhaps more protracted, by the lights of perverted science. Let us therefore brace ourselves to our duties, and so bear ourselves that, if the British Empire and its Commonwealth last for a thousand years, men will still say, "This was their finest hour."

Chapter 8

The Battle of Britain, RAF Kenley

Excerpt from Winstons Churchill's speech, House of Commons, 20 August 1940.

The great air battle which has been in progress over this Island for the last few weeks has recently attained a high intensity. It is too soon to attempt to assign limits either to its scale or to its duration. We must certainly expect that greater efforts will be made by the enemy than any he has so far put forth. Hostile air fields are still being developed in France and the Low Countries, and the movement of squadrons and material for attacking us is still proceeding.

August 1940

We flew down to Kenley on 29 August, refuelling in Yorkshire, and landing in the afternoon where we were shown to our quarters. We knew Kenley, of course because we were there before we went to France. The CO, Group Captain Prickman was still there and we began to prepare for the next day. I know I slept well that night and woke up ready for the fray. As I record this sixty years on, I cannot remember all the hours that we flew or whether it was in the afternoon or in the morning, so I have deferred to my Log Book which, when I look at it even now, puts a lump in my throat just thinking about it. Our first day was 30 August and we were up early, bright-eyed and ready to go. We couldn't have been more ready to get stuck into the enemy. Little did we know what would happen to us over the next few weeks.

We took off on our first flight in the morning. We were ordered to fly to 15,000 ft on a set course. The whole squadron took off, every serviceable aircraft. At 18,000 ft we ran into a lot of enemy aircraft, Me110's and Bombers. The squadron sort of broke up and we didn't attack any huge number of aircraft, instead the Me110's were attacking us. I found myself coming in head-on, to a Messerschmitt 110, which I knew was a fatal thing to do since they had much better armament than us, two 20 mm cannons and four 8mm machine guns, so I broke downwards. The next thing, I was on my own. One thing we had been told was that if you were on your own – don't stick around. So, I was turning around to go home, when I suddenly saw a German aircraft, a Heinkel 111 on its own because its squadron had been attacked and had broken up and it was on its way back across the Channel. I immediately turned, made a quarter attack and fired all my guns into it. I set both engines on fire and it came in with no motors. I followed it down and stopped shooting at it because it obviously couldn't get home; I watched it make a good landing in a field with its wheels up. I then saw the crew get out, one of whom was being carried because he was very badly wounded. When I got back to Kenley, I reported to the Intelligence Officer, Pilot Officer Henry, and by that time the rest of the squadron had already arrived back or were arriving back.

My Log Book shows that I flew again in the afternoon on that day but no engagement with the enemy. At the end of that day, we had lost Pilot Officer Jenkins, old Jenks who had been with us since Perth, Pilot Officer Francis who had been flying with Tom Gleave, and Sergeant Dickinson. We found out in the next few days that they had all been killed. My Flight Commander George Brown had been shot down, injured and was in hospital in Aylesford. Squadron Leader Starr, the CO; Pilot Officer Samolinski and Flying Officer Wedgwood had all been shot at and shot down but were uninjured, only their aircraft were out of action. After one action, we had lost seven aircraft; over half our flying squadron of twelve. Pilot Officer Carthew – 'Tweedle Dee' never flew again as far as I know. It upset him so much he couldn't fly anymore so he was posted elsewhere.[2] Sergeant Dickinson had baled out of his aircraft and was shot dead by Me109's as he came down by parachute.

The next day, August 31, my Log Book tells me I flew only one sortie. I was 19-years-old and not very fond of writing, so my Log Book shows a mass of 'scrambles' with no real story behind them. Had I known at the time that the Battle of Britain was to go down in history, I would have made a much better effort at recording every detail. Anyway at the end of that particular day, we were told that Squadron Leader Starr had been killed. Like Dickinson, he too was shot down while coming down by parachute. Squadron Leader Tom Gleave took over and was shot down and very grievously burnt the same day. Tom survived the War but was in and out of hospital for skin grafts for many years. We stayed in touch with one another after the War despite being many thousands of miles apart and we remained great friends until the day he died.

The squadron now was without a Commanding Officer. With both Squadron Leaders' Starr and Gleave gone and Flight Commander Georgie Brown in hospital, Bill Cambridge, who was 'B' Flight Commander, took over as CO of the squadron. The following day, 1 September, I flew twice. During the first flight, we ran into a very

---

2. Carthew shared claim for a Dornier on 11/09/40 and was subsequently posted to 85 Squadron later that month.

large formation of Dorniers and Me110's. In my Log Book I have recorded one of the Dornier 215 as a 'probable' kill. We went into line-abreast, and after one attack I broke away, I could not see any of the squadron after that so returned home not having joined up with anybody. When I got back I found that Pilot Officer 'Curly' Clifton had not returned. 'Curly' and I had been through Perth and Brize Norton together, he and Jenkins were two of my best friends. Jenkins had been killed on the first day at Kenley and I found out later that 'Curly' too had been killed. By that time I was getting very nervous. I couldn't eat until near the end of the day and had developed a nervous tic in my left eye. I used to live on tomato juice for breakfast and lunch, but ate a good meal at night when it was all over.

The next day, 2 September, I flew twice again and during that day we lost Flying Officer David Bell-Salter and Sergeant Metham, both were shot down and finished up in Halton Hospital. Bell-Salter had a very lucky escape. He baled out of his stricken aircraft and deployed his parachute – which didn't fully open. However, he survived the fall with only two broken legs because he landed in a tree.

I flew another two sorties on 3 September, and on that day, 'Elsie' Murch was shot down. He baled out and landed in a Laundry at Tunbridge Wells. Four of us paid a visit to him in hospital and could barely get into his room for flowers, fruit and chocolates.

By now, fighter pilots were in short supply so we were getting volunteers from bomber squadrons. Flying Officer Truman, a Canadian who had trained on Hampden bombers, was one such volunteer. He was given just ten hours of training on a Hurricane before joining us. Poor chap was killed on 4 September.

Pilot Officer Samolinski was shot down on 5 September, his aircraft was a write off but he got out safely. On the 6 September I flew on two sorties, and our Acting Squadron Leader Bill Cambridge was killed on one of them. So, we were without both Squadron Leader and Flight Commander until we were given Squadron Leader Edge from 605 Squadron as our CO.

I was given two days off and decided to go and see some of our pilots who were in Halton Hospital. There were three of them in hospital there, Georgie Brown, David Bell-Salter and Sergeant Metham. Metham had been very badly burnt while the others had broken limbs and bullet wounds. This was the worst thing that I ever did because I arrived there as they were bathing Sergeant Metham who was covered in gentian violet. The bones over his eyebrows and his nose were showing through the skin because the flesh had all been burnt away and his hands were like claws. The other two were covered in plaster and bandages. I spent a couple of hours with them, handing cigarettes to them and taking them away because they couldn't hold them. All this frightened me considerably.

The next day I came back and started flying again I will always remember 9 September. It was the best attack that the squadron had ever done, because for the first time we had a really good Squadron Leader – Gerry Edge, who had come from 605 Squadron. We took off in the afternoon, only nine of us because we could not put twelve aircraft in the air, we had lost too many aircraft and they had not been replaced quickly enough. At about 20,000 ft we saw thirty or forty enemy aircraft, Ju88's, flying towards us on the beam. Gerry Edge immediately formed us in line-abreast, all nine of us, and we turned into these aircraft from about a mile away. We met head-on. It was a most frightening attack. I was in the middle, flying as Edge's No.2, unable to break either right or left. The only way I could go was either up or down. When I thought of going up (all this was in a split second – no time to think clearly) they would get me underneath straight into my balls and I could not think of that as an option! I knew if I pushed my stick forward my engine would cut out, for when you push the stick forward in a Hurricane, the engine immediately cuts. I fired a burst at the Ju88's, which were coming towards us at a great rate of knots, and then, at the last moment, I pushed my stick forward and the enemy went over the top of me by a few feet. It really was a terrifying attack. When I came out of my dive, there were no aircraft around me so I returned to Kenley.

After a fight with the enemy, the whole squadron would be broken and I don't ever remember forming up again, it was amazing how few aircraft were to be seen after a scrap. Sometimes two or more could join up, but no orders were ever issued as far as I can remember, the sensible thing was to return to base as low down as possible. Being on your own and climbing back towards the enemy was a recipe for disaster. From 10,000 ft and above, the Thames was the best landmark. When forced low, after an escape from the enemy, the landmarks I remember best were the long straight railway line from westwards from Ashford across Kent; Canterbury Cathedral, (with Thomas a Becket waving to us!) and the masts at Fareham Radar Station. We couldn't read the names on Railway Stations as they had been removed.

We did not know how many aircraft we had shot down because things happened so quickly; nobody knew who had shot down what. I made no claim. When German Records were examined after the war however, we discovered that in this one attack, nine of us got five of those Ju88's. All were confirmed and credited to 253 Squadron. So, I was credited with a half of a Ju88. There were all sorts of claims made during the 'Battle', many of which were found out to be quite untrue. I find it impossible to believe those Hurricane pilots who claimed to have destroyed ten-fifteen enemy aircraft. The Me109's speed, manoeuvrability and armament, plus their advantage in height to attack us, was too good for our fighters. Check some of the books our pilots have written and their claims against the Luftwaffe losses as disclosed by German records after the war!

So it went on. Flying Officer Watts was shot down on 9 September but he was uninjured. Then we had quite a good spell. I flew most days in September. On 14 September we lost Sergeant Higgins who was killed and on the twentieth we lost two pilots both injured – Sergeant Barton and Sergeant Innes. When Squadron Leader Edge was shot down on 26 September and finished up in hospital he was replaced by a fellow called Duke-Woolley who came from a Blenheim Squadron. He'd also taken us up on 15 September, which was to be the turning point in the Battle. We were scrambled to go to Angels 25 (25,000 ft), so he took the whole squadron up to 15,000 ft and stayed there, hanging around, with huge battles going on above us which we were watching. Aircraft were coming down in flames all over the place and I wondered why we weren't climbing to 25,000 ft! After half an hour at 15,000 ft, we came back down and landed. We found out afterwards that he thought that he *was* at 25,000 ft. I really rubbished him over that and made myself very unpopular with him and from then on my name was mud as far as he was concerned. Not that it worried me very much at that time.

The 'Battle' went on through the remainder of September and through October with much the same sort of things happening. It was gradually getting better though; there were fewer bombers and a lot more fighters. Duke-Woolley was an awful leader, so most times that we were scrambled, we either saw nothing, couldn't catch what we did see; or broke up and ran for our lives because we were being attacked from above. Because the enemy were doing all the attacking, they picked the height that best suited them and their largest attacks were in the morning and early afternoon with the sun behind them or above. I can tell you, I ran for cover as many times as I attacked. When they dived to attack us, the squadron broke. I used to turn in towards them, and dive flat out at the same time, making it impossible for them to take a bead on me; when I pulled out, I was usually on my own with a few 'dots' and smoking 'dots' around the sky. It was rare that we ever formed up again as a squadron. If we could have been airborne ten minutes earlier than we were, it would have made it a more even battle. The fact that we were more manoeuvrable was not an issue as they could dive on us and then climb away from us without having a dog-fight. It was only when they stayed to fight that things became more equal. I fired my guns very few times, but couldn't tell when as I had forgotten by the time I filled my Log Book in at the end of the month.

There were quite a few times we were vectored to bandits that failed to materialise. I would say one in three intercepts failed, because of (a) wrong height, (b) weather or (c) bandits turned back home. After a failed intercept we would await new orders from Control. Haze and cloud were the main factors. Ninety per cent of the time we met them, the enemy were above us. In those conditions our visibility was about 1,500 yds and quite often we did not see them. Bombers were at 15-20,000 ft, fighters were at 25,000 ft and above. On a good day without haze or cloud we could see them from twenty-five miles away. Mostly we were looking into the sun. There was very little cloud in September. In October there was more, mainly between 5-10,000 ft.

We nearly always had the Chief Controller from Kenley vectoring us, but we would like to have been sent off ten minutes earlier than we were when bandits were climbing to their heights over France. This always made us below them in height when we met them. After a failed intercept, if the weather was okay we would either be told to patrol between two towns (i.e. Ashford – Maidstone) at a certain height, or told to return to home base, depending on circumstances. In late September/early October, Me109's came over between 25-30,000 ft. This was far too high for a Hurricane's performance, so we were nearly always at a disadvantage and we didn't bother to attack.

As I recall, *Standby* meant being either in or at one's aircraft. *Readiness* meant sitting around dispersal waiting for the telephone to ring. *Available 15 minutes*, meant being in or around the Mess, or lying on one's bed, dozing. *Available 30 minutes*, was much the same as above, but one could be anywhere on the station. When on *Available*, the Tannoy would broadcast in the Mess, bringing either flights or squadrons to readiness. Transport would be outside the Mess to take pilots to dispersal, and usually we were ready to fly well within the allotted time. After returning from a sortie, we were met by the intelligence officer, to whom we gave all the details, meanwhile the aircraft were being rearmed, refuelled etc. This was all done in about fifteen minutes, providing there were no problems with the aircraft, and if necessary we took off after a cup of tea if not too urgent.

Our tactics remained the same throughout the 'Battle', four flights of three aircraft, in Vic formation, which could be either turned into either line-abreast or line-astern for attacking purposes. It showed no imagination, we discussed it several times, but nothing was done, because we were a badly savaged squadron and had lost six COs between 30 August and the end of September, either killed or wounded and of those six, there had been only one really good leader.

As a result of the experiences I had had in France, I learned a great deal about how to both attack and evade German fighters – which were a lot better than we had been led to believe. A combination of this experience and the fact that I had really good eyesight meant I was made 'tail-end-Charlie' during the 'Battle'. My role was to weave around looking for the enemy and report anything I saw to the Leader.

In mid-October we were equipped for the first time with VHF radio. The old TR9D HF sets were awful to listen to with all sorts of interference; it was better between aircraft and the ground than between aircraft. It was terrific and I went up on my own to 28,000 ft to test the maximum distance at which we could maintain contact. When we were fitted with VHF, I did an air test on 8 November. Shortly after that, the whole squadron were equipped. Some squadrons had already been equipped, so I would say 11 Group was done first in October and November, then 253 Squadron in November. HF and VHF were operating at the same time for a while. I remember going south to the coast seventy miles away and still getting wonderful reception after the TR9D HF sets. We had no serious bugs as I remember. At that height I was waffling through the air at eighty mph on the clock when four Me109's crossed just above me. I couldn't believe my luck, so I pulled the stick back hard and fired my guns, that was the straw that broke the camel's back because as soon as I fired my guns I stalled and spun down to earth. I had no idea whether I hit any aircraft so I did not claim any damaged.

During October and November, 253 Squadron used to take off about three times a week at dawn to fly to Hawkinge where we would spend a very uncomfortable day because the enemy, who were only Me109's and no bombers, were usually several thousand feet above us. Although I did claim a damaged Me109 on the twenty third. Twenty-five years after the War, German records show, a Me109

5212 was damaged and crash-landed at Bec-sur-Mer. RAF records show it could only have been me because I was the only pilot who had fired his guns at that time. We hated going to Hawkinge, all morning we were below the enemy and looking into the sun. Our aircraft and pilots that were shot down were just wasted because there were never any bombers.

So, to put my badly kept Log Book straight, the months of October and November were spent either seeing an empty sky, seeing the enemy too far away and unable to catch them, or breaking up and running away, as they dived us from above, for the total of NO bombers. We were all tired and a rest period would have done us the world of good. During the time from September to the end of November we lost yet more pilots: Samolinski, a Pole, was killed; Sergeant Allgood was killed; Sergeant Moore was injured. Dicky Graves and Sergeant Edgley were both injured and so it went on. Nowak was also shot down but he was unhurt

Towards the end of October 1940, 253 Squadron were stood down for the day at RAF Kenley. Jack Strang, Alan Corkett and myself, the only three remaining from the original Squadron formed at Manston in 1939, piled into my lovely 1934 Jaguar SS which I had bought for five pounds from Dicky Graves, who was recovering from burns after being shot down on 29 September. The three of us arrived in London, parked in Soho Square and went for a meal. I was so exhausted that I fell asleep into a plate of whale steak and chips. Then we went to see *Gone with the Wind* at Leicester Square and after that , with a few beers inside, us we ended up at the Paradise Club. In the early hours of the morning we staggered out to find my car and return to Kenley for dawn readiness. We eventually found the car and as we were pouring into it a policeman arrived out of the darkness and the conversation that flowed was as follows:

Policeman: "Good evening gentlemen, who is the driver?"

Me: "I am" – (spoken with great joviality).

Policeman: "Well, you have parked in a No Parking area for more than four hours with no lights on. Could I please see your registration?"

Me: "I'm sorry, I don't have one."

Policeman: "Are you insured?"

Me: "No, I'm afraid not."

Policeman: "Well then, do you have a driving licence?"

Me: "Oh yes" and with great gusto, I pulled it out and showed him.

Policeman: "Well, young Sirs, the Air Force are a bloody nuisance in London now, so please bugger off."

Which we did. And I am relieved to say we did not fly that day. As for the incident in Soho, I don't think the police would be so forgiving these days.

On 9 December, I was posted to No.5 FTS for a rest. No.5 FTS was a Flying Training School in Sealand on the Welsh/English border, about five miles outside Chester. I was sent as an instructor on single engine Masters. I was very upset because I did not want to leave the squadron. I tried my best to avoid being posted but in retrospect, I understand that they were doing it to everybody. At the time though, I thought that I had done something wrong and was being kicked out, it was a pity altogether that they did not give enough information on those things at the time. It would have been good to be told that I wasn't being expelled from the squadron, just in need of a rest.

Chapter 9

The Battle of Britain, In retrospect

Excerpt from Winston Churchill's speech, House of Commons, 20 August 1940.

The gratitude of every home in our Island, in our Empire, and indeed throughout the world, except in the abodes of the guilty, goes out to the British airmen who, undaunted by odds, unwearied in their constant challenge and mortal danger, are turning the tide of the world war by their prowess and by their devotion. Never in the field of human conflict was so much owed by so many to so few.

In retrospect, the Battle of Britain was not won by us; it was lost by the Germans. They were doing the attacking, so picked the height that best suited them and their largest attacks were in the morning and early afternoon with the sun behind them or above; I can tell you that I ran for cover as many times as I attacked. When they dived to attack us, the squadron broke. I used to turn in towards them, and dive flat out at the same time, making it impossible for them to take a bead on me; when I pulled out, I was usually on my own with a few 'dots' and smoking 'dots' around the sky. It was rare that we ever formed up again as a squadron. If we could have been airborne 10 minutes earlier than we were, it would have made it more even. The fact that we were more manoeuvrable was not an issue as they could dive on us and then climb away from us without having a dog-fight. It was only when they stayed to fight that things became more equal.

The Me109 was the best fighting plane of the three main types of fighters involved. It could out-dive and out-climb both Hurricanes and Spitfires. It was faster than the Hurricane at all heights and faster than the Spitfire above 23,000 ft. The armament of the 109 was far superior to ours since their 20 mm cannon was lethal at 1,000 yds. Our .303 peashooters were effective at 250 yards or less. The Hurricane's endurance was about two hours. In the squadron, most flights were an hour and forty-five minutes, which gave us fifteen minutes for landing difficulties. This included times of full throttle. We would almost always be on the climb when vectored towards 'bandits', which would be at full throttle. I cannot remember what the airspeed was, but think it was about 200 mph on the clock. Our ground speed was dependant on the wind speed and direction. The ammo load was 300 rounds each gun: 2400 rounds. We never used tracer, but about thirty per cent de Wilde ammo.

The only reason that they lost the Battle of Britain was the fact that the 109's could not stay over England long enough. In other words they did not have enough fuel. Their flying time allowed them to get to London, where they had ten minutes, then they had to return. Now, if they had had long-range fuel tanks, they would have won the 'Battle'. They had good armour plate, we had to be within a couple of hundred yards and hit with all our guns to shoot them down, whereas they could open-fire with their two cannons at a thousand yards and still make an awful mess of our aircraft.

However, we would have won the Battle of Britain in much better form and far quicker causing far greater casualties if our armament had been the same as the Germans'. Once again, it was the top brass in the Air Force that wouldn't listen to anybody, and thought that eight machine-guns would be the greatest armament of all. Well, they were proved wrong. After the Battle of Britain they immediately did something about it and from then on Spitfires and Hurricanes were equipped with cannon and machine-guns. Although, once again, they still carried on with .303 machine-guns whereas the Germans had .5, which was a much better machine-gun and did more damage. I remember coming back from one sortie where an armour-piercing bullet had come through the half-inch-thick armour plating behind my head, the armour piercing core came all the way through and stuck in the back of my neck. It didn't go in far, only through the skin and when I pulled it out I could prick my finger with it because it was as sharp as a needle. That was the difference between a .5 machine gun and a .303. In retrospect I am of the firm opinion that the Germans lost the Battle of Britain.

Looking back now, it is my opinion that we were treated disgracefully as a squadron and I cannot understand why Sir Hugh Dowding has got a memorial when things like that happened. The way he handled the Battle of France was not good. We lost far more Hurricanes than we should have done. We would have had more aircraft for the Battle of Britain if he had not thrown them away as he did in France. He split a squadron into two halves, without their CO and sent them to different places, only half trained at the time. When I look at it now, we had the worst aircraft out in France. We were the only ones without mirrors and without armour plating and yet during the time in France, and the subsequent Battle of Britain, we shot down a good many enemy aircraft.

The fact that not one of our pilots, many of whom served in both battles, was awarded a DFC is a disgrace. Up until November 1940, when 253 Squadron had shot down many German aircraft, not one medal had been awarded. Our losses had been severe. In fact we had one of the highest Squadron Casualty Losses, and the most in such a short period of time. We lost both Flight Commanders and our CO in France, reformed with a new CO and Flight Commanders before we went to the Battle of Britain, where we lost both Starr and Gleave, the Squadron Leaders who were with us, in the first two days. Then we lost our Acting Flight Commander and then, when we finally got a good one in Gerry Edge, he was shot down and we finished up with Duke-Woolley who had come from a night fighter squadron.

The Air Ministry asked Duke-Woolley to put forward two pilots in the squadron for DFC's. He put himself forward although he had done practically nothing with us and another pilot, who had come from 32 Squadron. He was the fellow who claimed to chase Messerschmitts, catch them after a hundred miles and shoot them down into the sea. We know now however, that it was absolutely impossible for him to have done that because a Hurricane couldn't catch a Messerschmitt in a month of Sundays. I suppose it was because we lost so many leaders that there was no one around to recommend anybody! Twice during the 'Battle', we were joined by a lone Hurricane OK-1, which we found out was Keith Park, Air Officer Commanding 11 Group. We had no complaints; at least it showed an interest in what we were doing. Well, as you can tell, I am still angry about it all, a very angry old man. For what they did to our Squadron as well as what they didn't do!

Ruth, Mother and myself at the beach (aged 12).

My first suit, 1937.

Myself, Mother, Ruth, Father and Betty in 1939.

Front cover of my log book.

EFTS Perth, April 1939, with Tiger Moth in background.

YEAR		AIRCRAFT		PILOT, OR	2ND PILOT, PUPIL	DUTY
MONTH	DATE	Type	No.	1ST PILOT	OR PASSENGER	(INCLUDING RESULTS AND REMARKS)
—	—	—	—	—	—	TOTALS BROUGHT FORWARD

ME - EFTS PERTH APRIL 1939

APO's BRAINWAITE + GREENWOOD. NO 2 F.TS BRIZE-NORTON, OXFORDSHIRE MAY - NOV 1939

GRAND TOTAL [Cols. (1) to (10)]
.................Hrs.................Mins.

TOTALS CARRIED FORWARD

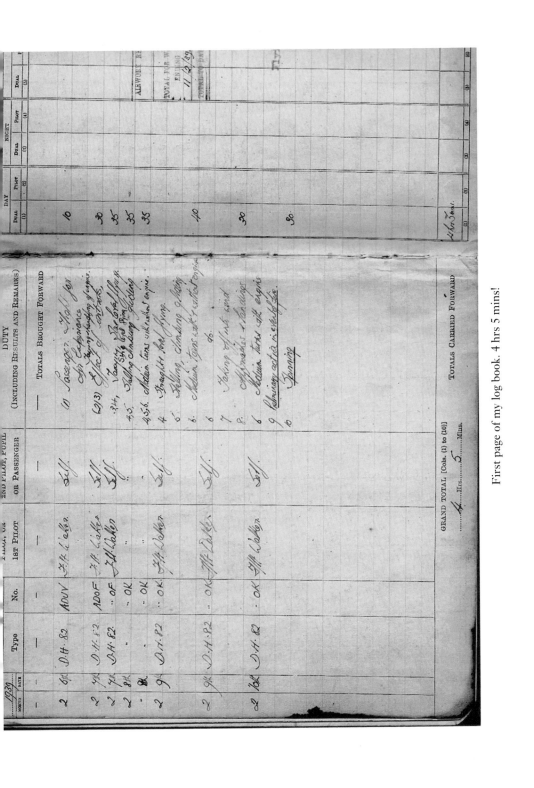

First page of my log book. 4 hrs 5 mins!

Photos from EFTS Perth, February–April 1939.

Airspeed Oxford. None of us knew what we would be flying at Brize Norton, but most of us hoped that we would be on single engined aircraft because that would lead us onto fighters. Two thirds of the course, myself included, went onto Airspeed Oxfords, which were the twin engined training aircrafts, and the other third went onto Harvards. I was very fortunate in the end because I was assigned to a fighter, I was far happier in a single engined aircraft and could see myself shooting down enemy aircraft right, left and centre! (Wikipedia)

Pilot Officers Corkett, Clifton and Dawbarn after receiving their wings. Brize Norton, December 1939.

2FTS Brize Norton Passing Out. Back row left to right.

Blank	
Sgt James	
Blank	
P/O Broadhurst	Posted 222 Sqdn Killed Oct 7 1940 B of B
P/O Deacon (Canadian)	
P/O Jeffries	Formed 253 Sqdn Posted to 3 Sqdn in B of B
P/O Spencer	
P/O Heywood	257 Sqdn B of B Pilot Killed Oct 22
Blank	
P/O Radford	Formed 253 Sqdn Killed May 19th in France
P/O Clifton	Form' 253 Sqdn Killed B of B Sept 2 1940
Blank	
P/O Wakefield (Canadian)	
P/O Hon. Child-Villiers	
P/O Bell-Salter	Formed 253 Sqdn Shot down and injured Sept 2 B of B
P/O Goldberg (South African)	
Blank	
P/O Mallet (Argentinian)	
Blank	
Blank	
P/O Ward	
P/O Murch	Formed 253 Sqdn Shot down Oct 11 1940 Killed in Nth Africa 1943
Blank	
P/O Brownlie	on Bombers POW 1943
P/O Dawbarn	formed 253 Sqdn Posted to 17 Sqdn for B of B
Sgt Marsh	Formed 253 Sqdn Posted to 238 Sqdn Killed in B of B Aug 1940
P/O Morton	
Blank	
P/O Prosser	
P/O Saville	
Blank	
P/O Ford	Formed 253 Sqdn Shot down & injured in France 18 May 1940 Lost Eye and Lung
Blank	
P/O Edwards	
P/O Jenkins	Formed 253 Sqdn Killed B of B Aug 30 1940
P/O Relton	
P/O J.B. Hobbs	Formed 253 Sqdn then to 3 Sqdn B of B Pilot Killed at Eladem 1941
P/O Angus Cameron (Canadian)	Killed at Sea 1941
P/O Williams	
P/O A.H. Corkett	Formed 253 Sqdn. B of B pilot
P/O Greenwood	Formed 253 Sqdn B of B pilot
P/O Bisgood	Formed 253 Sqdn then to 3 Sqdn. B of B pilot
P/O Machin	

Me the day after my "Wings" party.

P/O John Greenwood, 1940.

253 Squadron emblem, *Come one. Come all.*

Miles Magister. The Air Force had decided that they were so short of single-engine fighter squadrons that they were going to form four new Squadrons. Thinking we would be flying Hurricanes, we were delighted with the news, but when we went to see all these lovely Hurricanes, we found out that we only had two Miles Magister training aircraft! (Wikipedia)

Three weeks later we were equipped with, of all things, Fairey Battles. We were all thoroughly disappointed but were told not to worry, we'd only have the Fairey Battles for a couple of months, and then we would be re-equipped with Hurricanes! (Wikipedia)

Hurricane SWP with me in the cockpit taken at Northolt a few days before we left for France. This was the aircraft I had in France. "L" series, fixed pitch, fabric covering, no armour, no mirrors.

YEAR 1940		AIRCRAFT		PILOT, OR 1ST PILOT	2ND PILOT, PUPIL OR PASSENGER	DUTY (INCLUDING RESULTS AND REMARKS)	DAY Dual	DAY Pilot	NIGHT Dual	NIGHT Pilot	Dual	PASS
MONTH	DATE	Type	No.									
						TOTALS BROUGHT FORWARD	20·15	125·26		3·26	22·36	55
5	17	Hurricane	L1712	Self	—	Patrol of Douai + Cambrai at 20,000 ft. Met nothing		1·05				
	18	"	L1712	"	—	Patrol of afternoon. ditto to Dornier 215's escorted by 110 110s.		1·45				
						Shot dear one Do 215. Near Armies at Merville.		·15				
	18	"	L1712	"	—	Merville to Lille. Patrol of Lille, Roubaix, Douai		1·15			BATTLE	
	19	"	L1712	"	—	at 8,000 ft. met nothing. Took off to attack Me 109's and Dorniers. Caught them at 2,000 ft. near Cambrai. Shot down one Me 109. Crashed south of Lille					FLANDERS	
						Patrol over aerodrome, waiting for enemy bombers. Jas making Evacuated Lille, resigned to Kenley.		·15				
					—			1·10				
					—	Kenley to Hastings. Visited + accompanied 74 Blenheims to Calais area. Returned to Kenley		1·15				
	20	"	L1663	"	—	North to Hastings. Patrol near Calais. Contact + action this time in the evening. No action. Returned to Kenley		2·30			2nd	
	21	"	P2183	"	—			4·00				
						TOTALS CARRIED FORWARD	20·15	130·25		3·26	22·36	55

GRAND TOTAL (Cols. (1) to (10))
262 Hrs. 40 Mins.

The page from my logbook which records my three days in France and my first two victories, a Dornier 215 and a Me109. The Battle of France was a learning place, which I am sure saved my life later-on in the Battle of Britain. 262 hours and 40 mins.

The page from my logbook which records my third kill. A Me109 over Merville confirmed by "Curly" Clifton who was later killed during the Battle of Britain.

The 1927 Austin 7 belonging to "Curly Clifton" which ran on cigarette lighter fuel and carried up to nine pilots from dispersal to the Kirton in Lindsay Mess.

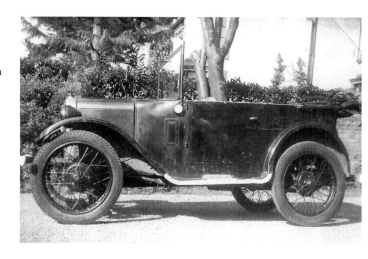

The He 111 which I shot down on 30 August 1940, following an attack on Farnborough aerodrome. The aircraft force landed at Haxted Farm Lingfield.

Me109E-3's of JG.26 during the Battle of Britain. The Me109 was the best fighting plane. It could out-dive and out-climb both the Hurricane and Spitfire. It was faster than the Hurricane at all heights and faster than the Spitfire above 23,000 ft. The armament of the 109 was far superior to ours since their 20mm cannon was lethal at 1,000 yards whereas our .303 peashooters were only effective at 250 yards or less. (Wikipedia)

MONTH	DATE	Type	No.	1ST PILOT	2ND PILOT, PUPIL OR PASSENGER	DUTY (INCLUDING RESULTS AND REMARKS)	DAY Dual (1)	DAY Pilot (2)	NIGHT Dual (3)	NIGHT Pilot (4)	Dual (5)
						TOTALS BROUGHT FORWARD	29.45	197.40 30.		6.40	
8	28	Hurricane	3412	Self	—	Operational Patrol					
	29	"	3414	Self	—	To Det. Flight for a/c firing. Ystegin. Dawn attacks		2.05			
				"	—	Fighter Recco		1.00			
	29	"	P3H4	"	—	Patrol to Kenley		2.30			
	30	"	P3H4	"	—	Scramble — shot down He III		1.00			
	3	"	3534	"	—	Scramble		1.10			
								20.05			
						Summary for August / Hurricane					
						Unit No 253					
						Date 3/9/40					
						Signature					
						O.C. 253					
						TOTALS CARRIED FORWARD	29.45	217.55			

GRAND TOTAL [Cols. (1) to (10)]
334 Hrs. 15 Mins.

My logbook for the first three days at RAF Kenley which records the Heinkel 111 shot down. 334 hrs 15 mins.

Squadron Leader Harold Starr came from 245 Squadron and, like all our C/O's, he had no battle experience. He took over from Tom Gleave who took over again after S/leader King left us. This unsettled the Squadron as we all liked Tom Gleave. However he settled in quite well and was eager to learn from us. On August 29 the Squadron moved to Kenly to join the Battle of Britain. On the morning of August 31 he was killed and replaced by S/L Gleave who was shot down and badly burnt in the afternoon. He was replaced on September 1 by F/Lt Cambridge who had been "B" Flight Commander. He was shot down and killed on September 5 and replaced by Gerry Edge.

Squadron Leader Tom Gleave had been in a desk job, but had been pulling all the strings he could to get into a squadron. Although he would have loved to 'hit the Hun over Dunkirk', he realised the totally traumatized situation of 253. With himself and both flight commanders having never seen any enemy action and half the squadron with only a few hours on Hurricanes, he relied on the few of us still left from the French debacle to help train the remainder of the pilots.

Many portraits were made of pilots during the Battle of Britain. This one was of Squadron Leader "Gerry" Edge who came from 605 Squadron and was our first CO who had experienced enemy action. He was quite a feisty little man and took no nonsense, and was easily the best leader that 253 had since its formation. He was shot down in the Channel on September 26 and hospitalised.

Squadron Leader Harold Starr.

MONTH DATE	Type	No.	PILOT, OR 1ST PILOT	2ND PILOT, PUPIL OR PASSENGER	DUTY (INCLUDING RESULTS AND REMARKS)	DAY Dual	DAY Pilot	NIGHT Dual	NIGHT Pilot	INSTRUMENT Dual
					TOTALS BROUGHT FORWARD		134·55			
9 1	Hurricane	P3194	Self	—	Dornier. Do 21. probable.		·50			
2	"	P3194	"	—	Scramble.		·20			
3	"	P3194	"	—	"		·55			
				—	"		·40			
				—	"		1·00			
4	"	P3194	"	—	"		3·0			
5	"	R2658	"	—	"		1·15			
6	"	R2658	"	—	"		1·00			
				—	"		·35			
				—	"		·45			
9	"	P3037	"	—	Sgt. Hood missing - so to 88.		·55			
14	"	R2686	"	—	" Dogfighting "		1·00	←		
10	"	R2686	"	—	"		1·00			
				—	"		1·00			
13	"	N2353	"	—	"		·10			
13	"	N2353	"	—	"		1·00			
17	"	Y6671	"	—	"		·35			
15	"	N2353	"	—	Scramble.		1·05			
13	"	N2353	"	—	"		1·20			
14	"	N2353	"	—	"		1·05			
25	"	N2353	"	—	"		1·00			
				—	"		1·00			
				TOTALS CARRIED FORWARD		130·35			

GRAND TOTAL [Cols. (1) to (10)]
.....356 Hrs. 55 Mins.

My log book for most of September 1940 which records the Dornier I shot down on 1 September which I claimed as a probable. The arrow on 9 September highlights the day on which the Squadron made a head on attack, with nine of us securing five of those aircraft that were later confirmed, after the war. It was also the day on which we were credited with half of a Ju88 each. I annotated my log book in 1965 after the 25th anniversary reunion. 356 hrs 55mins.

This Ju88 was one of five shot down by 9 aircraft of 253 Squadron in a head on attack on the afternoon of the 9 September 1940.

253 Squadron taken shortly after I left in December 1940. L to R, sitting on wing: Sgt. RA Innes, P/O RC Graves – unknown – unknown – P/O DA Pennington – P/O DS Yapp. L to R standing: F/O AF Eckford – Capt. de Scitivaux – F/O SR Peacock-Edwards – P/O G Marsland – F/Lt. RM Duke-Woolley – S/Ldr Walker – F/Lt. RF Watts – F/O Wall (Adjutant) – F/O Henry (Intelligence). L to R sitting: Sgt. AS Dredge – unknown – Sgt. EHC Kee.

MO/YR DATE	Type	No.	PILOT, OR 1ST PILOT	2ND PILOT, PUPIL OR PASSENGER	DUTY (INCLUDING RESULTS AND REMARKS)	DAY Dual (1)	DAY Pilot (2)	NIGHT Dual (3)	NIGHT Pilot (4)	Dual (5)
	—	—	—	—	TOTALS BROUGHT FORWARD		224.55			
10 9/11	Hurricane	L928	Self	—	Scramble		1.5			
	"	V7499	"	—	"		1.20			
	"	"	"	—	"		.45			
8	"	P2172	"	—	Air Test		.55			
12	"	V7499	"	—	Scramble		.25			
13	"	V7499	"	—	"		1.20			
	"	V7499	"	—	"		1.06			
15	"	V7499 / L1208	"	—	18,000 ft. fired at 4 Me109's, but stalled and spun (600 ft o'clock)		.10			
	"	V7499	"	—	Scramble		.45			
17	"	V7499	"	—	"		1.30			
19	"	V7499	"	—	"		1.00			
	"	V7499	"	—	"		.05			
19	"	V7499	"	—	"		1.30			
	"	V6499	"	—	"		1.10			
20	"		"	—	"		1.30			
21	"		"	—	"		.35			
23	"	V7499	"	—	"		.20			
	"		"	—	"		.10			
	"		"	—	"		.05			
29	"	10172 / V7499 / V1312	"	—	Test / Scramble / Test		1.25 / .10 / 1.00 / .45			
					TOTALS CARRIED FORWARD		260.45			

GRAND TOTAL [Cols. (1) to (10)] ..387.. Hrs. ..05.. Mins.

My log book for much of October. It records the day I met four Me109's and stalled while firing. 387hrs 5 mins.

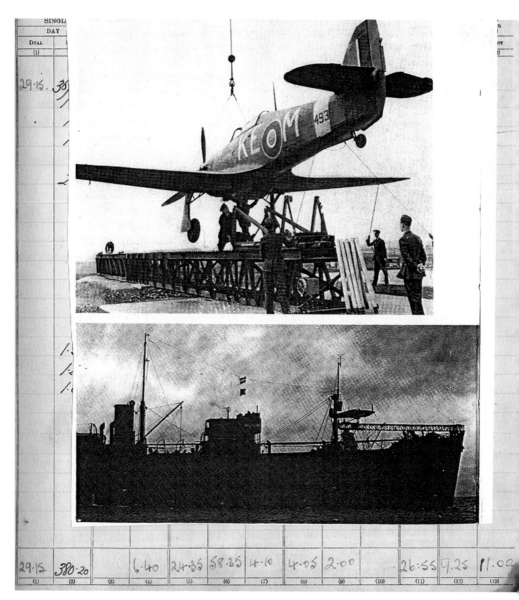

A photo of the experimental catapult at Farnborough and my catapult Hurricane on the Empire Flame, which I kept in my logbook.

The Battle of Britain 25th Anniversary Reception, London Guildhall, 1965. I am on the right of the boxed area just under the left wing of the Spitfire with Angela Gleave and Alan "Corky" Corket and Tom Gleave.

60th Anniversary of the Battle of Britain. With Guy Harris, 253 Squadron, Commander of B Flight who was shot down and badly injured during the Battle of France.

50th Anniversary Battle of Britain, 1990, Stanmore. I am third from the left.

1942 Month	Date	Type	No.	Pilot, or 1st Pilot	2nd Pilot, Pupil or Passenger	Duty (Including Results and Remarks)	DAY Dual	DAY Pilot	NIGHT Dual	NIGHT Pilot	Dual	Pilot
					—	TOTALS BROUGHT FORWARD	—	438.35				
2	5	Master	N7338	Self	St. Abbott	To Abbott		.45				
	6	Hurricane	W9?22	"	—	Local flying		.45				
	7	"	A.G.22	"	—	Dog-fighting		.10				
	10	"	"	"	—	Formation		1.00				
					—			1.00				
				POSTED TO 6.5 Sqdn (FARNWOOD) COMM.								
	17	Hurricane		Self	—	Fuel Recco		1.05				
	20	"		"	—	Formation + Air firing		1.00				
	21	"		"	—	Flaming Bactre		1.16				
	24	"		"	—	Camera Gun Practice		.50				

Sailed for India at 6.15 Sept. March 17th
1942 on "Johan van Oldenbarnevelt"
from Capetown. Had 21st birthday on board in
Freetown, got very drunk + left to bed by
Nicholson VC

GRAND TOTAL [Cols. (1) to (10)] 576 Hrs. 0 Mins.

TOTALS CARRIED FORWARD   446.30

My twenty–first birthday....got very drunk and sent to bed. 576 hrs.

MONTH DATE	Type	No.	PILOT, OR 1ST PILOT	2ND PILOT, PUPIL OR PASSENGER	DUTY (INCLUDING RESULTS AND REMARKS)	DAY DUAL	DAY PILOT	NIGHT DUAL	NIGHT PILOT	1ST PILOT
					TOTALS BROUGHT FORWARD		475.15			
12 8	Hurricane	X	Self	—	to Imphal & return		1.20			
9	"	M	"	1	Jorcomte to 29,000		1.40			
10	"	M	"	1	Jorcomte to 19,000		.55			
11	"	K	"	1	to Imphal		.60			
12	"	K	"	—	Coca and Imphal		1.35			
				1	Imphal to Mandalay		.40			
					return with to Bishops					
		K.	"		Imphal to Zen		2.45			
14	"	G	"	1	to Rangos & return & ho & go		1.30			
					hat and taple.					
15	"	K	"	1	Jorcomte. Nothing seen		2.30			
18	"	K	"	1	Akerata. cancelled		.55			
19	"	J	"	1	Jorcomte. Nothing seen		.16			
20	"	G	"	1	to Chittagong. Ken to Nape		1.15			
					enter Arrn. One Blenhein shot					
					down Afr. Vehicles R.O.O 10 Mall					
21	"	1.	"	1	to Chittagong Ken to Akyab 105.		3.45			ENGINE CUT
					tached go of the books enely of Con					NORTH SH
					R.Gas					got back
					Jo Basra					by sand
27	"	E	"	—	Jo Basra		2.25			
28	"	E	"	1	Ben Abanta		.16			
							.16			
					TOTALS CARRIED FORWARD		491.56			

GRAND TOTAL [Cols. (1) to (10)] 627 Hrs. 0 Min.

The page from my Log Book which records my forced landing at Cox's Bazaar. 627hrs.

INDIA 1943

India, 1943.

India, 1944.

Pilot Officer Colin Francis' burial service in 1981 at Brookwood Cemetery, Surrey. Francis joined 253 Squadron after France, and was posted as missing on the first sortie, 30 August 1940. He was not found until forty years later when he was dug up from a field. Lest we forget.

Fassberg, Germany, 1946. Standing in front of a Tempest II. Fourth from right. We used to fly under the bridges down the Kiel Canal, they were very high so it didn't take much to fly under them!

Guinea Airways flight to Kangaroo Island 1953. I am third from the right next to Joyce.

The Greenwoods, April 2000. From left: Michael, Joyce, Nicholas, John, Christopher and Helen.

My service medals. My Battle of Britain medal is on the left and my recently awarded Russian Arctic Convoy medal is on the right.

At the Battle of Britain monument, The Embankment, 2005.

With a painting of the He111 I downed in the Battle of Britain. Painted by Chris Bramley, son of John and Margaret Bramley, good friends and neighbours in Shoalwater, April 2012.

Chapter 10

Posted for a Rest

59 OTU, RAF Turnhouse, January 1941

Although I was posted to No.5 FTS for a rest in December, I was only there for a week when the whole of 5 FTS was posted to Turnhill because Sealand was to become an OTU for Spitfires. Meanwhile, I was making myself into the worst Instructor they had ever had. I used to go to the Chief Flight Instructor every day to see if I could get posted back to the squadron, I was making myself as unpopular as I possibly could. Eventually, on 20 January, I was posted to a new OTU – No.59 – which was forming at Turnhouse near Edinburgh, where we had been with 253 Squadron five months before. When I got there, I found out that our CO was a Wing Commander Ira Jones, DSO, MC, DFC and Bar, MM, which he had been awarded during the First World War – he was one of the Aces of the First World War, in 74 Squadron. There was only him, myself and 'Fanny' Orton, who had been a pilot with 73 Squadron in France, and who had been shot down there in May 1940. He had been badly burned and had only just come out of hospital; he was pretty scarred and burnt around the face and hands. We became very great friends.

There were only the three of us for the first week. We had no aircraft for the first few days then got a couple of Hurricanes but no pupils and no other instructors, so 'Fanny' Orton and myself used to go into Edinburgh every night, get pickled and really enjoy ourselves. So did old Ira Jones who was a great character. He had a tremendous stutter, and he loved the women; he escorted the most gorgeous women. We would join him at the North British Hotel when we saw him there; we'd sit down, have a drink and ogle his ladies and dance with them. Anyway we really enjoyed ourselves there, so much so that one night 'Fanny' and myself were walking down the street from the North British Hotel, towards Fanny's car (an open racing sort of a car – Triumph, if I remember rightly) and there was a drunken sailor a few yards in front of us, staggering down the road; we saw a lady come out of a shop door and say something to him and in very loud Scottish voice he shouted, "Get awhay wi' ya, ya dirrty whoman" which I have always remembered because it was hilarious.

While we were at Turnhouse, we were getting drunk nearly every night and often got up to high jinks. While the Desert Campaign was on and the British were making their first move in North Africa, through Messa Matru and Benghazi, 'Fanny' and myself decided to play the desert campaign on the carpet of the Officers' Mess. We got two buckets of sand and a bucket of water, mixed it all up and made the most terrible mess there – it was supposed to be the Western Desert. Well, the next day we were marched in front of the Duke of Hamilton, who was the Station Commander (it was he who Rudolph Hess flew to Scotland to see). He was very annoyed and he put us under 'open arrest' which meant to say that we were confined to the camp.

It so happened that the next day, we had been invited by the Navy to go over the battleship 'Prince of Wales' which was in Rosyth Dock. We decided that nobody would know if we slipped out at night to visit the battleship, so that's what we did. We toured the 'Prince of Wales', got very happy on pink gin in the Wardroom then came back; like stupid fools, we broke the Mess up again. The next thing, we were under arrest, 'close arrest' this time. A Summary of Evidence was taken and we were sent down to see the AOC (Air Officer Commanding) who was at Worcester, which is a long way from Edinburgh. We went down by train to Worcester and The Group Headquarters was in the Workhouse and there we stayed the night, whether at a Hotel, or the Workhouse or the mess there, I cannot remember. The following morning we were marched, separately, before the AOC and were both given a reprimand, which was all right really because it did not mean loss of any seniority. We immediately returned on the train from Worcester back to Edinburgh. We drank at the bar all the way up there, so by the time we got there we were squiffy, again. We arrived back at Turnhouse to discover that we were moving down to Crosby-on-Eden. A few more pilots had arrived.

What we did was to fly the aircraft down to Crosby-on-Eden which was near Carlisle, then get in a station wagon, three or four of us, and come back to Edinburgh, stay the night there and the next morning fly another Hurricane down until we had moved all the aircraft down to Crosby-on-Eden. By this time quite a lot of Pilot Instructors had arrived, nearly all Battle of Britain pilots, some of them I kept in touch with until they died – one being Donald Stones (Dimsie), Bob Oxspring, Overton, La Rue, Dunning-White all, well-known names. The CO was a fellow by the name of Fullergood, a Group Captain, and I was a Supernumerary Flight Commander until 20 May, when I volunteered for Merchant Catapult ships.

We had lots of fun while at Crosby-on-Eden. The days were spent flying – including a lot of low flying down the Solway Firth – and most nights were spent in Carlisle I remember one night, me and another pilot picked up a couple of girls. The night went really well and it looked like our luck was in. The other pilot had an Austin 7 and, at the time, this seemed the ideal place to end the evening 'romantically'. We soon discovered, however, that it was impossible to have sex with your legs sticking out of the window.

At that time, I had a 'Standard Avon Special' 1934 Model which I had bought from Dickie Graves for five pounds after he had been shot down in 253 Squadron in October – it was the original Jaguar called a Standard Special which gave the initials SS to the cars following. 'Dimsie' Stones had the SS Saloon 1935 Model with a great big long body. One night, we drove back from a night out in Carlisle. I was driving flat-out following 'Dimsie' when I got into an uncontrollable side spin, weaving all around the road, until the car suddenly turned around twice on its axis. I did not turn over fortunately, because it was a very low-slung car, but I burst all the tyres on it and had to leave it on the side of the road then get new tyres for it the next day. I also remember a couple of us pulling some Very cartridges to bits (usually they are two great charcoal lumps which are either red or green or in a certain colour that lights up when fired) and we took these out and went out over the roofs of the huts because Crosby-on-Eden was a new station with only wooden huts built just as a wartime station; it was not as comfortable as a peace time station and it was pretty cold in the winter. They used to have big pot-bellied fires in the rooms. We went along the roofs then any chimneys we saw with smoke coming out we dropped one of these Very cartridges down. They'd go into the fire and make a tremendous amount of smoke and flame and scare the daylights out of you if you were sitting near the fire. As I remember, we were told off by the Group Captain Fullergood over that, but he was pretty good bloke altogether, he let lots of things pass.

When he was the Station Commander at Debden, Fullergood had been involved in a strange incident and that's why he was up at Crosby-on-Eden. He was the CO at the station when a Heinkel 111 landed at Debden by mistake one night. Thinking it was in Germany, it landed and taxied up to the Tower then, realising that it had made a mistake, it taxied out again and took off. Fullergood was blamed for that because he was Station Commander and it should not have taken off again.

I was getting brassed off and wanted to get back to a squadron to get back on operations – they were doing 'rhubarbs' over France at that time; dropping below cloud level to search for opportunity targets such as locomotives and trains, aircraft on the ground, enemy troops and vehicles on roads. Then a signal came around to all units asking for volunteers to join a new unit being formed called 'Merchant Ship Fighter Unit', which was still in in its highly experimental stages. A Hurricane MkI fighter, which was then considered expendable, was to be fired off the bow of a merchant ship of about 5,000 tons by means of a rocket loaded trolley on which the aircraft sat. This sounded highly exciting so I volunteered, together with my mate 'Dimsie' Stones but Dimsie never made it because he got posted to another squadron. He had seen one of his old mates – flown over and seen him – and he got him onto his squadron, so I went down on my own. I did not see 'Dimsie' again until I met him in India later on, in 1943. I was the only one from Crosby-on-Eden to go down to Farnborough. The idea behind Catapult Ships was to tackle the Focke Wulf Condors, which were large four-engined German Bombers, which were going out into the Atlantic from Stavanger, in Norway , then returning South and landing in Bordeaux, France. Their job was to sight convoys and then give information to the U-boats about their position. They also carried bombs and were going down convoy lanes at five hundred feet dropping bombs and causing much damage and consternation amongst the Merchant Seamen who didn't seem to mind torpedoes but hated bombs!

Chapter 11

Catapult Ships

RAE Farnborough, May 1941

I received my orders on 20 May, which were to proceed to Farnborough for the first firing of the catapult across the airstrip. Since there were no Hurricanes fitted up with the gear at the time they were using a Fairey Fulmar. I packed all my gear into my rakish sports car which, because I had no registration or insurance, had been filled up at the bowser with 100 octane aircraft fuel plus a couple of extra four gallon cans of fuel to get me there. With a monumental hangover from my farewell party the night before, I left for Farnborough where I arrived that evening and went to bed dead tired.

The next day I met two other pilots who had also volunteered, a fellow called Ford and a New Zealander called Spurdle, who were Seven and Eight crews and I was number Nine. Spurdle was due to go that morning followed by Ford and myself in the afternoon. We all went out to the airfield together to find a Fairey Fulmar on the catapult. None of us had ever flown one before, although I had flown Fairey Battles with 253 and the Fulmar was similar to a Fairey Battle in the cockpit. We inspected the catapult trolley, which was loaded with thirteen cordite rockets, each about six feet long by three inches in diameter. The catapult itself was held to a back stanchion by a strip of steel three inches wide by a half an inch thick and when the rocket fired this strip snapped clean in half and the trolley took off at a rate of knots which gave the pilot in the cockpit a kick in the neck of 3G. The pilot rested his head on a thick pad fixed to the armour plating behind his head with the elbow of the hand holding the control column firmly stuck into his thigh. The rails were about 18 yards long and the trolley came to a sudden halt when it hit the buffers at the end, by which time the aircraft was just under take-off speed; but with the ship's speed and also turned into wind would, hopefully, give us the take-off speed. The Fairey Fulmar sat on the catapult with its wheels down and just off the ground so after firing it would bounce onto its wheels and hey-ho you were off!

Spurdle sat in the cockpit, was shown all the 'tits and levers' and was finally ready. He started up and after warming the engine gave it full throttle. He then signalled the firing officer in his little cabin that he was ready and in three seconds there was a most tremendous bang, a flash of flames, the trolley whizzed down the rails and the aircraft was bumping over the field and airborne. I looked at Ford, he looked at me, and together we both said, "Jesus, what have we got ourselves into?"

Ford was the next off, but by the time the aircraft had been loaded onto the trolley the weather had closed in and it was deemed unfit for flying so we retired to the Mess to drown our sorrows. At the same time on the radio we heard that over a thousand souls had drowned their sorrow for the last time as HMS *Hood* sank beneath the waves after engaging with the Bismarck.

I did not get much sleep that night waiting for the big moment the next day but exactly the same thing happened with the weather, so only Ford got off, leaving me to spend another sleepless night. Next day it was my turn. With much trepidation I ran the motor up to full throttle and gave the signal, got ready, and suddenly there was a most enormous acceleration and noise and I momentarily blacked out and woke up bouncing across the field half stupefied. I flew around for half an hour during which time I flew low over my parents' house in Borden near Farnham where they were living after being bombed out during the Battle of Britain.

The next day we were to move to Speke, near Liverpool, which was to be our home station. I thought I would go and pay a visit to my parents and spend a day with them before I left, so I got Ford to take my luggage and his, and drive my car up there while I went up by train the next day. We got up to Speke and the CO there was a real character from the First World War. He was a New Zealander called Louis Strange and earned a DSO in the last War by having his plane turned upside down and not being strapped in; he had hung onto the handles of his machine gun until the plane came upright again! In this War (he had not flown since the last War) he had flown a Hurricane back from France instead of breaking it up with an axe. There was nobody else to fly, so he had taken it and was awarded a DFC for it. Anyway, he was a fine gentleman, he was our CO and everybody was very pleased.

Well we spent the next two months at Speke. We flew a little and I had a couple of weeks leave and went home. When I returned to Speke, I teamed up with a fellow called 'Durex' Kendal who became a good friend of mine. He was nick-named 'Durex' because his name was Kendal, from which went to Rendell (which was a female foaming contraceptive) and so went to 'Durex' a name that stuck until he was killed the following year. We found two very nice WAAF girlfriends, my young lady was called Anne Halliwell, she was a lovely girl. We used to go out with them and take them around in my car, and did all the things that girls and boys do. The Air Force gave us £50 each to buy civilian clothes, I spent mine on a pair of green silk pyjamas, which cost about twelve pounds, and the rest I spent on booze and night clubs. Thank you very much Air Ministry.

Now, I had those green silk pyjamas until the Christmas of '44 in India when, having got very drunk the night before, we played a game called 'The Blue Flame' in which you put your legs up around your neck and you light your farts. When it was my turn I singed my beautiful green silk pyjamas so badly that they just crumpled and fell to bits where all the singe marks were.

The Catapult Ship to which I had been allotted was called the *Empire Flame*. It was still being completed at Cammell Laird Shipyards in Birkenhead on the other side of the Mersey so one day I went over there to inspect it and found that it would be at least four weeks before it was to be completed. Meanwhile we were just playing around, nightclubs and cinemas and generally enjoying ourselves. Towards the end of July, the *Empire Flame* was ready and was about to do its trials in the Clyde, so it sailed up from Liverpool to the Clyde. Meanwhile, I flew my aircraft up to Abbotsinch, which is the Airport just south of Glasgow. From there they loaded the plane onto the ship while the ship did its trials and I was fired off in the aircraft. My Flight Direction Officer was a Naval Lieutenant, a Canadian by the name of Lieutenant McKinnon. We steamed down the Clyde, and when the time came, they turned into wind, I gave the signal, braced myself and McKinnon put the switch over. Flash, bang and off I went, straight down the end of the ship, to get speed up. I did not go up straight away but just dropped down in front of the bow so that I could gather speed, just above the water, then started climbing. It scared the living daylights out of the poor old skipper, he thought I had gone in the drink because he could not see me but everything was all right and I landed at Abbottsinch. They reloaded the plane, and I went back on board and that's when the Skipper told me that he thought I had gone "in the drink". He was a great bloke, he treated me like a son and was very afraid that I might have done myself some damage. The First Officer was named Cross; he was a stocky little chap and very nice with it, as was the Chief Wireless Officer or 'Sparks' as he was known. In fact all the crew seemed to be friendly and I thought this is going to be quite a good trip.

Chapter 12

The Empire Flame

July 1941

On 30 July we sailed out of the Clyde. I was on the *Empire Flame* and 'Durex' Kendal was on the *Empire Ocean*. We had a convoy of around seventy or eighty ships. We sailed right up The Minch to the North of Scotland and then started going West towards the south of Iceland at the speed of the slowest ship, which was about nine knots, because it took us twenty-one days to get to Halifax. It was a boring old trip in so far as there was nothing to do on board really except inspect the Aircraft and make sure everything was at the ready. The food was magnificent – we used to have for breakfast, fruit juice, cereal, waffles and maple syrup then bacon, eggs, tomatoes, kidneys – you name it, there was everything there, then rice and haddock and as much coffee as you wanted and it was a really great breakfast. At night I used to play poker with the First Officer, the Skipper and the Chief Wireless Officer or 'Sparks' as he was known. One day I fixed the cards so that when they were dealt them that night, one player would have three Kings, another would have three Aces, another would have a fill-in for a Straight and I would have nothing. They would all have to draw one or two cards while I threw my hand in and it ended up that one had a Royal Straight Flush, one had four Aces and one had four Kings. Because the sailors weren't paid a whole lot and they were bidding up to ten pounds (which was twice their week's wages), 'Sparks' and the First Officer were sweating. In the end they had to show their cards and the Royal Straight Flush won it, which was 'Sparks', he was very happy until I told them that I had fixed all the cards!

Sometimes I would go up onto the Bridge, the Skipper was very kind, I could go up there whenever I liked and he taught me how to use the Sextant to work out our position, which was most interesting.

I had to look after a crew of four airmen and McKinnon, the Naval Lieutenant, had two Naval Ratings – they were torpedo men and they looked after the catapult, whereas my four ratings looked after the aircraft. I had an armourer, a fitter, a rigger and an instrument maker, and I made sure they were well looked after. When the seas were not too wild, I used to sit in the aircraft about every hour-and-a-half and run the engine up, to make sure that the motor was warm and ready to take off. Other than that I had very little to do so once we had passed the tip of Greenland I did not even have to run the motor up because there was no chance of being attacked by a Focke Wulf and we weren't equipped to fly against U-boats, which was just a waste of time. I unloaded some of the ammunition out of the guns, taking ten rounds or so out of each of the eight guns. I had a .303 rifle so used to pop away at birds and porpoises and things in the water until I was quietly told it was not the accepted thing to shoot down an albatross or to hit porpoise.

When we got to Halifax, Nova Scotia the RCAF unloaded my aircraft and 'Durex's' aircraft and ferried them over to the Royal Canadian Air Force station there where they repainted them with anti-corrosion paint and inspected them. We flew them there a couple of times. By then it was the month of August and it was holiday time; there were lots of sailing boats in the harbour so we used to go and fly low over these boats and pull the stick hard back so that the slip-stream would blow them over. That was about the only fun we had there. There were no pubs, you had to go to a hotel, and then go to a liquor store to buy your liquor, which is what 'Durex' and myself did. We used to drink our liquor in our room, which wasn't much fun. It was really a boring old week. Even now when I look back on it, it was still boring – Halifax was not much of a town and we were quite happy to get on our way back home again.

Once again it was a slow convoy. Off we went, and once again we got back without any ships being sunk in either convoy and of course we saw no Focke Wulf Condors, they obviously had heard all about us and they weren't making any more attacks on shipping. When we got about ten miles off the coast of England near Liverpool, I was to be shot off early in the morning and was to land at Speke so I pulled out my radio and loaded all the contraband that I and my crew had, plus what the Naval Lieutenant and his crew had; nylon stockings and things like that were contraband. I brought forty pairs of nylons back and, at the end of the War, my mother and sisters still had some pairs unused – that's how good they were. I also gave some to my girlfriend, Anne Halliwell. I was fired off and landed at Speke in radio silence, which caused quite a furore, so I stopped a rocket from the CO but that was all. After that the ship went down the Manchester Ship Canal to Manchester without stopping off at Liverpool and I had to go down there to pick up my gear and take all the crew's contraband with me. After this I went on a week's leave.

When I got back I was told that my next ship would be a ship called the *Novelist*, which was an old steamer built in the First World War with a single high stack and that it was going to Savannah in Georgia, USA which I thought was great. I soon realised however that the *Novelist* was a different proposition from the *Empire Flame*; her crew had been gentlemanly people who appreciated what you were doing for them. The Captain of *Novelist* thought we were up-starts, he did not like having us on board and he did not like having the aircraft on board, so we started off on the wrong foot. I can't even remember any of the crew of that ship, that's how it played on me. Anyway, she was heading to Savannah in the USA, which was not at war so we did not worry very much, or at least I didn't. We sailed in October and once again we went out in a large convoy, ours was the only catapult ship in that convoy of ninety-six ships. Thirteen days out, well out of the danger area, we left the convoy and headed South making out towards Savannah, where we arrived twenty-one days after leaving Liverpool.

Savannah is on the River Savannah, about four or five miles inland, up a winding, marshy old river. As we sailed up it, we noticed little smoke fires burning everywhere along the banks which, I was told, was where the bootleggers were distilling their illicit liquor, whisky and hooch. Within no time at all after arriving at Port, I had my fingerprints taken because I was a foreigner, all ten fingers were taken and I am now recorded as a civilian in America because I was signed on as an Assistant Steward. As the Customs Officers went off, a man and a woman came on board, very nice people, who had met the Canadian Pilot on the last trip, so they were waiting for me to arrive. They took me home with them and I flew around in an aircraft, a single engined, high wing monoplane, a Piper Cub and saw the city from above. I stayed the night with them and went out to breakfast the next morning – the first time I had ever been out to a restaurant for breakfast. I had never seen people going to breakfast in restaurants. That night I slept on the ship as we were supposed to do and all night negroes were loading it with resin and timber chanting and singing as they were loading. It was 'Take it down to Hell, raise it up to Heaven' all night, I did not get a wink of sleep, so I decided that the next day I was going to stay at a hotel on my own, because my Naval Lieutenant had gone home to Windsor, Ontario for a few days and planned to meet the ship at Halifax. I went to the De Soto Hotel where there was a very large swimming pool and, although it was October the weather was still hot, so I got into my bathers and went for a swim; I had the pool all to myself. As I swam, I saw this fellow standing on his own, watching me, and as I got out he walked up to me and we started talking. I told him that I had come in on a Catapult Ship then I asked why there was nobody else swimming in the pool and he said it was far too cold, the swimmers had packed up a month ago. I couldn't believe it. His name was Gaydi Toombs and he was Vice President of the De Soto Hotel. We got on really well and he gave me a suite for which he would not let me pay. I went around with him the whole time I was there. He introduced me to a girl who was supposed to be a debutante, she was a nice girl, and we went around together and had a great time.

Seven days later we were loaded up and ready to sail to Halifax and re-join the convoy which was about a three or four day journey. Off we went down the river and arrived in Halifax where we stayed a day, then the following day we left in convoy, about sixty ships. Once again the convoy was very slow, about twelve knots. We were a few days out of Halifax when my Corporal in charge of my crew came to me and told me that the Captain had ordered him to put my crew and the two Naval Ratings on submarine watch. He asked if I knew anything about it, I said that I didn't. I knew that all merchant seamen were paid extra to go on submarine watch so I asked him if he would be prepared to do it if he and the crew were paid and he said yes. I went and saw the Captain and told him that he had approached my crew without first seeing me; telling them they were to go on submarine watch, which was inappropriate. He said that as Captain of the ship, everyone was under his command and that they would do submarine watch otherwise he would put them in irons. I said: "Very well, in that case you will put me in irons because I have told them not to do it, unless you pay them as you pay your crew, then they will do it". We had quite an argument. He did not put me in irons because he realised that he would be in a great deal of trouble, especially if a Focke Wulf appeared on the scene (we were just getting into the area at that time) so nothing was done. We did not say very much to each other after that. Meanwhile I lived on their grotty food; everything we ate on that ship had weevils in it. All the bread, all the porridge, anything with grain whatsoever and we lived on stews and porridge – awful food, completely different from the *Empire Flame*. I was very glad when we got to the end of the trip. I had just about had enough of Catapult Ships with people like that on board, I did not enjoy it one little bit. The final episode came when we arrived in port and a Naval Captain came on board because, apparently, our skipper had already told the Navy about what had happened between us. We had a long discussion over who was in charge of my crew and who wasn't and I called the skipper a little pipsqueak. I finished up deciding at the end of it all that I was not going to make any more trips on catapult ships so when I got back to the station I went to Louis Strange and said that I wished to apply for a posting and he arranged it for me.

In retrospect, Catapult Ships were a great scheme, the way it was thought up and done so quickly. Unfortunately though there were the Captains of ships who resented the fact that you were on their ship and in charge of the RAF crews. I spent six months from May until November on these ships. It remains in my memory as quite a pleasant one, except for that last ship, *Novelist*, and even then it was quite pleasant because I did go to America and I enjoyed myself there.

When I settled back in England, I said goodbye to my lovely girlfriend and I sold my car to Spurdle, who was shot off at Farnborough two days before I was. Funnily enough, fifty years later I met him at our Battle of Britain reunion in England in 1990, having not seen him since 1941. I asked him: "How did my car go?" and he told me it was the best buy he had ever made. I had sold it to him for five pounds, which is what I had paid for it a year before.

Chapter 13

55 OTU Usworth, November 1941

After I got back to England, I went on leave for a fortnight. I was absolutely fed up to the back teeth. All I wanted to do was go back to Ops. On the Catapult Ships the only time I had been fired off was when I got back to England – we never saw a single enemy aircraft and now here I was back in OTU's, right back where I started. I made up my mind that I would make such a bloody nuisance of myself that they would soon post me somewhere else. There I stayed until my posting came through which was to a Hurricane OTU at Usworth near Newcastle.

I didn't get chance to say goodbye to my old friend 'Durex' who had just gone off on his third trip across the Atlantic. He got back as they started Russian convoys and he was on the *Empire Morn* when Ju88's carrying torpedoes attacked the convoy. 'Durex' was fired off the ship on the North Cape of Norway, shot down a Ju88, circled the crew who were in the sea, then went up and bailed out. They are not quite sure, but they think he may have hit the tail when he jumped out, because his parachute had not opened completely. They pulled him out of the water a matter of two or three minutes after he landed but he had broken a lot of bones and died on board shortly afterwards. My poor old mate; his family should have received a medal, at least a DFC if not a DSO but he got nothing. He served in the Battle of Britain, got nothing there and he got nothing in Catapult Ships and he gave his life for it. I thought that was dreadful. What was upsetting was the fact that, of all the people who were involved with

Catapult Ships, my mate 'Durex' Kendal was the only person that was killed.

From Speke I went to Usworth in the North East. I was there from November 1941 until February 1942 during which time I was a fairly bad Instructor and was very pleased when I was posted to 615 Squadron based at Fairwood Common in South Wales as Supernumerary Flight Commander. The Chief Flying Instructor at Usworth was Squadron Leader Lambert. He used to go to his room, lock himself in and play the violin for hours. An ambulance came to take him away one day and we never saw him again, poor chap.

The flying conditions at Usworth were very bad; they should never have had an OTU there. It was an industrial area and there was always a haze in the sky; most of the time the visibility was only about 1,000 to 2,000 yds. It was all right once you got to a few thousand feet above the haze, it was lovely then. One day I was instructing two pupils in formation flying in Hurricanes when the visibility got worse and there was no way I could think how to get down; then I saw a hole in the clouds and I dived for it thinking they were with me. When I got under the clouds I found that the two pupils had not come with me and I felt very bad about that. I landed at Acklington, north of Newcastle. Apparently they got back to Usworth all right, but when I got home I copped a terrible rocket, as well I should have done. However it helped to get me posted the next week, and that was when I went to 615 Squadron, at Fairwood Common. We were only there for a short while before we heard that we were going overseas. Nobody knew quite where but we were all hoping that we were going to the Middle East. It turned out that we were going to India. Our CO was Ron Duckenfield; our Flight Commanders were Bob Holland and Dave McCormack who was an Australian.

We were given a week's leave so three of us, Bob Holland, myself and another pilot, Jimmy Gillies, decided that we would spend our week on the River Thames at Maidenhead. We spent a very drunken and funny week there. We were thrown out of our first hotel and had to move into another one. We drove around the town in a coach pulled by two horses and a coachman. Then I was caught in bed with the manageress of the local cinema, so we were all thrown out of our hotel so we moved across to the Thames Hotel and there we stayed for the rest of our leave until we went back to Fairwood Common.

Chapter 14

615 Squadron, Jessore, India

February 1942

In February the Squadron moved up to Liverpool by train and we boarded a big old Dutch Liner the *Johan Van Oldenbarneveldt* and joined a convoy that had a battleship, an aircraft carrier and quite a lot of destroyers. We started on our way up through the Minch, out into the Atlantic due West until south of Greenland, then South to off the coast of Brazil and then East across to Freetown where I had my twenty-first birthday. If you could think of a worse place to have your twenty-first birthday than on a troop ship off the port of Freetown in West Africa, I couldn't. Anyway, Jimmy Gillies and myself got very drunk and I was apprehended going through the corridors of the ship with a forty-five colt automatic looking for a drunken seagull. I was sent to bed, locked in my cabin and the next morning I was given a rocket by Nicolson VC who was on the boat and told me that when we arrived in Cape Town I would be Duty Officer and remain on board.

Well in a week's time we duly reached Cape Town and when everybody went off the ship, I stayed behind with one or two other people who also hadn't done the right thing. However, I decided that I wasn't going to stay there, so I went off and for the next four days nobody noticed that I was not there! I went to shore with different people and had a great time including with a very nice girl from Pretoria. She had a big Packard car and introduced me to a South African brandy called Van de Hume. Altogether, I had four very fine days in Cape Town. After we sailed, we lost most of our escort as they went off to invade Madagascar so we were left with something ridiculous like two Corvettes as we made our way up to Bombay. By the time we arrived in Bombay we had been at sea for five weeks with pretty much no female company because there were well over a thousand troops on board and only about ten females, most of them nurses.

After arriving in Bombay, our squadron was transferred onto another ship to Karachi. It was a two day trip and on board were fifty Queen Alexandra nurses and boy was it a change-round. There were now five nurses to every pilot and five Sisters to every Officer-pilot, so we had a very pleasant two days. When we arrived in Karachi, we were sent to the RAF Airfield where we discovered that the Hurricanes that should have come in the convoy with us were Spitfires and that our Hurricanes had gone to the Middle East. So the ship was then sent off to the Middle East with the 'Spits' and we had to wait for our Hurricanes to arrive back from the Middle East.

We were in Karachi for two or three weeks doing nothing except going to the Yacht Club and getting up to mischief. The first thing we did was to get measured for bush-jackets, shorts and shoes. We then threw away all the gear the RAF had issued us with because it was terrible: a great big heavy topee made of lead by the feel of it; Bombay bloomers, which came down to below one's knees, and very coarse khaki shirts. The clothes and shoes we had had made were absolutely dirt-cheap we couldn't believe it. We also each had a bearer which cost us thirty Rupees a month and we were not allowed to pay more (Rupee being worth one shilling and six pence).

We also went into Karachi, a big city that had what looked like blood-stains all around the roads. I thought, "My God, they must commit murder here", but it was caused by people spitting out the betel-nut with Lime that they chewed, covering the roads with a red stained spital. We spent most of our time at the Yacht Club, which was very pleasant. Some of us sailed, others just sat in the sun and drank and listened to music while spending our money. I got a terrible dose of what seemed to be dysentery and when I saw the doctor, in a very weak state, he said that there was only one thing for it and gave me a large glass of castor oil, which he made me drink on the spot because I would not have drunk it otherwise, and I spent the next two days on the toilet. I was not allowed to eat during that time and was only allowed soup for a couple of days after that. Thankfully, I recovered fairly quickly.

There was this road that ran through the aerodrome in Karachi that was used by the inhabitants of a village about a mile on the other side of the aerodrome. They used to grow watermelons, and then load them onto a big flat-bed truck which was pulled by a camel. They would then drive their cart to Karachi and sell their goods. Once they had sold everything they would turn their cart around and, as the camel knew the way back to the village and there were no branches, the driver used to lie on the flat-bed top and go to sleep. One day, as they came through the aerodrome, we turned the camel and cart around in the middle of the road and it just carried on walking until it ended up back in Karachi again. I don't know how the driver felt when he woke up.

At last our Hurricanes arrived and were assembled. We test flew them and we were all ready to go over to Bengal, to a place called Jessore which was about sixty miles north of Calcutta. During the time we had been there, Burma had fallen and the Japanese were at the gates of India so the day we left, a Blenheim arrived to lead us. The squadron followed the Blenheim and we landed at Rajpur to refuel and then to Delhi, staying the night. The next day we took off again to Allahabad, and then to Calcutta. We ran into a most tremendous rainstorm, visibility was poor and we had to fly at about 200 ft, eventually we landed at Jessore which was a large field in the middle of nowhere. However, we all arrived there without incident, parked our aircraft and were driven to our living quarters. The quarters consisted of bamboo huts with a dirt floor and a charpoy bed (a wooden frame with rope mattress) which we eventually found were all full of bugs. The Mess was a large bamboo hut with trestle tables and our food consisted mainly of locally bought chickens about the size of pigeons, eggs which were about half the size of an English egg, baked beans, dehydrated potatoes, dried eggs, dried milk. Really it was not a very flash diet.

Of course, there was no electricity so when we retired and went to bed we worked by hurricane lamp and put a mosquito net over our charpoy to keep out the mosquitoes, which flew in large, voracious formations. I remember one night we were playing poker by the light of the hurricane lamp on the table when a huge beetle came flying in, straight into my eye – armoured-plated these things were – and dropped upside down on the table. The beetle was half the size of my hand and I got the most tremendous black eye out of it.

Another thing I remember is low flying over the tops of the trees and one incident in particular. I was just flying locally out of Jessore for an hour's low flying practise, when a Vulture flew up out of the trees and went straight into my starboard wing root. Being so low over the trees, I was fortunate that I did not crash. When I landed, there was a huge hole, a lot of mashed blood and bone and this revolting neck hanging down, caught on the jagged edge of the wing.

We didn't do a lot of flying there because of the weather but in that time I got Dhobi itch, a prickly heat that went septic. I was very raw up under the arms and around the genital and I had ringworm.

I got all these three together; I was a mess. Eventually I got rid of the ringworm with Zambuk, while the other symptoms did not go until the monsoons broke. I remember standing out in the *freezing* cold rain. It was just wonderful after all the steaming heat. I was at Jessore for about four weeks before they split the squadron up and posted us to different places because the monsoon season put paid to any fighting

I was posted to, or attached to rather, Army 4 Corps Imphal, for the monsoon season, which lasted about two months. I made my way up there by train to the Brahmaputra, where we boarded a boat at a place called Miranshah and went up the river for two days until we got to Gauhati, which is a little village on the other side of the Brahmaputra. This was the beginning of the railhead and from there I caught a narrow-gauge train to a place called Dimapur. This was the start of the road through the mountains, through Kohima to Imphal. I went by road in an Army truck driven by an Indian driver, the most terrible ride I can ever remember. He was an awful driver and there were precipices going down 1,000 ft on either side of the road, it was the most awe inspiring but frightening ride.

Chapter 15

Army 4 Corps, Imphal

The road between Dimapur and Imphal was about 100 miles long and half way between was the village of Kohima, which was the centre of a big battle later in 1943-44. Imphal was the capital of Naga territory in a valley behind the Naga Hills and the headquarters of 4 Corps. I reported to Lieutenant General Scones who was CO of 4 Corps and was told that I would accompany Brigadier Gilpin, the Chief Engineer, in a Jeep to site aerodromes in the Imphal Valley. Brigadier Gilpin's rank was equivalent to an Air Commodore while I was just a lowly Flight Lieutenant but he seemed a very nice chap so the difference in rank did not seem to matter very much. Within four days we loaded our Jeep up and off we went into the wilds, as it were, for all the roads were dirt roads, some of them no better than tracks covered in water, and there was no way of getting through except by Jeep. We located areas for new aerodromes because Imphal was the only operational aerodrome at that time. Palel was one that I remember.

While Brigadier Gilpin and I were touring the Imphal Valley siting dromes, 4 Corps was transferred to Jorhart, which is in the middle of the tea gardens of Assam, on the plains north of Imphal. We went back to headquarters and moved with them to Jorhart. Once we were settled in we went round siting airfields in northern Assam. One day, we were driving in an open jeep down a muddy track (which became more like a stream during the monsoons) when suddenly a tribe of monkeys, as big as us, came out of the jungle and stopped in the middle of the road. Brigadier Gilpin and I looked at each other and decided that if the monkeys came towards us, we would have to drive straight through them. They looked at us, but fortunately went off into the jungle on the other side of the road.

There were the most beautiful butterflies you've ever seen in your life flying around in that area; gorgeous colours, huge things. Then we came out of the jungle and into paddy fields where we came across a bungalow, right in the middle of nowhere – it was a tea-garden. We stopped and met the manager who was a Scotsman, Mr. McKenzie. We stayed there for two days. He had a radiogram, a vast store of whiskey, gin, tonic and soda and every classical record, both opera and symphony, that you would wish for. So we sat there for a whole day and through the night listening to the music and drinking Long Chota Pegs.

The first night, as it was getting dark, I went outside and down the bungalow steps to have a pee and I almost stepped on a huge king cobra, a Hamadryad! So I rushed back into the lounge room and I said to McKenzie: "God, you have a huge cobra on your doorstep!" To which he replied, "Oh, that'll be George, he comes in when we play music and listens to the music curled up on the front step there". He staggered out, well and truly drunk, and picked this huge snake behind the neck and carried it about a hundred yards into the tea garden, where he dumped it and then returned to the bunglaow.

We left the next day, out into the paddy fields again, sited a couple of fields and eventually arrived back in Johart where we rejoined 4 Corps. There was not a lot to do so I spent most of my time staying with the tea planters, in particular Mr and Mrs James and their little child, very nice people. I was staying with them one day while a couple of Americans flyers were also there. I remember that one of them was from Wyoming and he said that if I had the day off, they were going over the Hump (Himalayas) to Kunming in China and returning later the same afternoon, and I could go with them if I liked. I said that I would like that, since there was nothing doing.

Next morning I was there bright and early to meet them, but the weather was not very good; a monsoon was raining off and on all the time and the cloud base was '10/10s' , (solid cloud) at about 500 ft, so I thought that this was going to be a dicey old trip. Anyway they said to get on board so I jumped up on board and found the whole aircraft was full of forty-four gallon drums of 100 octane fuel. At this point, I thought I had done a stupid thing by agreeing to the trip, what chance did they have with all that fuel on board? There wasn't really any backing out, so I sat up in the front with the pilot and co-pilot and we eventually took off.

Practically straight away we went into cloud between 500 and 1,000 ft, climbing up in it until about 17,000 ft then coming out of it above a great layer of cloud, which was absolutely beautiful because there were some peaks of the Himalayas sticking up through the cloud, it was very dramatic. After a while the cloud dispersed and it became really clear over China, so we had no trouble landing at Kunming. I had never seen anything like it. Chiang Kai-shek was building a new runway and there must have been a million coolies in a long line, perhaps a mile long, each one with a basket on his or her head. Each basket had a couple of stones in it, they were picking up the stones a quarry and walking about a mile to the end of the runway and dumping them there. That's how they were building the runway. Manpower was absolutely nothing to them and at that time there was not a lot of heavy machinery.

We offloaded our cargo and took off again after lunch for the return journey and it was good weather over China until we got over the Hump, then we were back into the cloud. I was nervous of descending through all the cloud, but we came down out of it at about 1,500 ft over the Brahmaputra in the middle of the tea gardens, so it wasn't too bad at all.

After that trip I didn't volunteer to go on any more. I used to go over to the Planters Club most days or nights, which was a very nice club, catering for the planters in a radius of about forty or fifty miles. One day I was sitting there and Mr James, who I had been staying with, asked me if I would walk outside with him. When outside he said, "John, I am embarrassed to tell you this, but you have very short shorts on and when you sit down your balls stick out from underneath and all the ladies are talking about it, I thought I would give you a warning." I said, "Thanks very much." I was highly embarrassed!

I stayed there until mid-November during which there wasn't very much to do. We liaised with the American Air Force as none of our Air Force were up there at all, they were all further down further South. One day one of the officers said there was a Lysander due to land on the Polo Field and we were to take part in an exercise that involved picking messages up from the field. So the Lysander duly came in and I met the crew. We erected two poles, about twenty feet high, with a cord across and the message tied to the middle of the cord. The Lysander flew low across the field with a hook hanging down to pull up the string and lift the message into the aircraft. After a couple of unsuccessful attempts, they met with success and they went away happy. So it went on, until mid-November when I got the call to go back to 615 Squadron

Chapter 16

615 Squadron, Feni

November 1942

The Arakan offensive had started as the monsoon was finishing. The Squadron was back at Jessore, so once again, I went down that terrible road through Kohima to the railhead at Dimapur, then from the railhead down the Brahmaputra on a ferry for about a day until we came to Jamshedpur. It was then by rail to Calcutta and back to Jessore. No sooner had I got to Jessore than we moved to Feni, which was much closer to the Burmese border. It was also a much bigger aerodrome with a long concrete strip, which had been built during the monsoon. It was a much better aerodrome and we started to operate from there.

Most of the time we were operating for the army over the Arakan, 'shooting up' Ferry steamers. There were no good targets except the odd steamer and bullock carts; we couldn't see any Japanese at all. They were well and truly camouflaged or hidden and we would just go and shoot up these boats, watch people diving overboard as we fired at them with four 20 mm cannon. I could not see much point in it at all; but I was only a lowly Flight Lieutenant.

One time, we had to go to Imphal to escort two squadrons of twin engine Bisleys, (they were the latest type of Blenheims) to Mandalay. We watched them bomb Mandalay while we escorted them. It looked a mess from the air, great clouds of smoke and dirt shooting up. We did not see any fighters and we came back again. Then we did an escort from Chittagong to Magwe for another squadron of Bisleys and there, right over Magwe, one of them received a direct hit from an ack-ack gun. It was the leading Bisley and went up in a great ball of smoke and flame and fell out of the sky. At the same time we saw some Japanese Zeros in the distance. I fired at one from a great distance – I did not see anything so I don't suppose for a moment that I hit it, but there was no way we were sticking around because we were no match at all for Zeros. We were virtually cannon fodder. We had four cannons and long-range tanks, which gave us a speed of about 180 mph. They ran rings around us, we could only dive for the ground and run away. Fortunately the Bisleys returned without losing any more to the fighters.

On 20 December, information came through that there were a lot of Japanese aircraft on Akyab airfield. We were given a moment's notice to fly to Chittagong, refuel, and then shoot them up on the airfield. So, we all took off as a squadron, landed to refuel and we were off. We flew low over Cox's Bazaar right the way down the coast until we got almost to Akyab, then the squadron was put on line abreast and we went straight over the airfield. I never saw any aircraft at all but heard that others had seen them. We all broke up as the Japs were firing heavy ack-ack which were bursting over the field at about 500 ft and it was a bit uncomfortable.

When we broke up I was on my own over Akyab Island on my way back to Chittagong when I saw this Japanese soldier in uniform making camouflage netting, right in the middle of a paddy field. I did a steep turn and came around, at the same time he saw me and started running for the ditch, but I gave him four cannons full so he never quite made it. Then I carried on my way North, flying at 50 ft along this beautiful white sandy beach which ran the whole way up to Cox's Bazaar and Chittagong; one of the most beautiful beaches in the world. I was flying along there just above the sand, when suddenly my cockpit filled up with smoke, and the engine stopped. I did not have time to put wheels down or anything like that, so I landed on this lovely beach with my wheels up, not doing myself any harm except hitting my shins as I got out of the aircraft with my parachute and helmet. On board we had what was known as a very secret IFF (Identification Friend or Foe) and there were two little buttons, so that if one had force-landed in enemy territory, one had to press these buttons that blew it up. So I pressed the two buttons and nothing happened, so I had to get my screwdriver out and remove the little electronic set. I then set off down the beach carrying it.

There I was, trudging down the beach in helmet, flying boots, khaki shorts and shirt, carrying this IFF set. I did not know exactly how far away I was from Cox's Bazaar but I must have been about thirty miles, I guessed. Walking along this beach towards night fall, a couple of natives came out of the jungle. It was a peculiar landscape. There was this beautiful beach and then it went up about a thousand feet in a jungle-like cliff. These two boys took me to their village. They spoke English so I told them what had happened and asked them if they could go up the beach a few miles and inform the army for me. The army was south of Cox's Bazaar, about twenty miles away. I had on me a belt with fifty rupees in silver, as we all did, so I pulled the belt off and gave them the fifty rupees, which made them practically millionaires, and off they went. I stayed there in their village hut for the night, feeding on bananas and curry and they looked after me very well. The next day, towards midday, an army truck came down to the beach with a couple of army officers and picked me up and took me back to Cox's Bazaar. First of all to their camp then in another truck to RAF Cox's Bazaar.

At that time RAF Cox's Bazaar was just a Cipher station with two officers there, both ex-bank clerks, and their only transport was a powerful Norton motorbike. They signalled my squadron at Feni that I was okay and my location and received a signal back saying that a Lysander would come and pick me up the following day – Christmas day, 1942. I had to go out and mark an airstrip for them to land. The only transport I had was this motor bike but I had never ridden a motor bike in my life before, so I got on this thing and was shown all the 'tits' and told what to do and what not to do. I had to travel about four or five miles from where they were so off I went. I was not very comfortable at all on this great juggernaut down the dirt roads, and when I went to decelerate, I turned the handle grip the wrong way and really took off! I hit a bank and went over the handlebars; I did not hurt myself very much, but had wrecked their only means of transport. I then walked the rest of the way, marked out the field as best as I could, and walked back and told these two poor old officers that I had messed their bike up. Anyway, they were very good about it and the next day the Lysander came and picked me up and flew me back to Feni.

I arrived there just before Christmas dinner and proceeded to get well and truly pissed. We all did, as a matter of fact, and we finished up pranging the CO's car, an American Chevrolet, on the corner of a bridge – Dave McCormack was driving it at the time. The CO, Ron Duckenfield, was not very happy about it, but it was soon repaired – only a bit of a dent. A couple of days later I was sent off with a Sergeant Pilot, with me leading, to do a reconnaissance of the Rathedaung to Akyab Island Road. The two of us were stooging along at about 1,000 ft when we got to the end of the road at Akyab, so we turned around and were on our way back when suddenly we ran head-on into six Japanese Zeros which were fifty feet higher than us, fortunately they had to turn to get behind us. Meanwhile, we had dropped our long-range tanks, pulled our emergency boost and were down on the treetops on the edge of the hills, weaving in and out of the trees for dear life. We were trying to stop the Zeros from getting a bead on us; after about ten minutes we lost them and they gave it away. When we arrived home the rest of the squadron tried to kid us that they had been Mohawks. Well I can assure you they were not, for they had the great big red spots on them and they followed us and fired on us – plus there were no Mohawks in the area.

A couple of days later, Ron Duckenfield led the squadron on a shoot up of Magwe Aerodrome. I was not with them that time, but they copped a lot of flak and Duckenfield was shot down. We did not know at the time but he was actually made a Prisoner of War (POW) and he served the rest of the War in Changi Prison. Dave McDonald, an Australian, took over the squadron and a couple of days later I was posted as a Flight Commander to 17 Squadron. Somebody flew me into Calcutta and I left a lot of very good friends behind.

I never saw Jimmy Gillies again, he was killed on Wingate's second expedition behind the lines in Burma; Bob Holland survived the war but died a few years later in a mid-air collision. Dave McCormack was killed in Imphal a year later after leading a flight of Spitfires into a monsoon cloud with four aircraft and three pilots lost. C'est le guerre!

Chapter 17

17 Squadron, Calcutta

1943

The Hurricanes of 17 Squadron were based on the Red Road, which was a road right in the centre of Calcutta with statues on either side of it. It was operating as an aerodrome because the Japanese had bombed Calcutta. They only dropped a couple of thousand pounds of bombs but two million people had evacuated! It was a difficult road to land on because it was bevelled, quite short and there were birds, Kite hawks, hovering over each end. The CO was 'Bush' Cotton, an Australian, and the other Flight Commander was named Bachelor. I took over 'B' Flight.

I arrived in Calcutta two days early so I decided to stay at the Great Eastern Hotel before I reported to the squadron. No sooner had I settled in there than I met another Battle of Britain pilot who I had been instructing with, Johnny Redman. His father was very high in the Church in Newcastle upon Tyne but Johnny was completely irreligious. We got well and truly stuck into the grog and decided late that night to go to Corio Road, which was the brothel area of Calcutta. As we got out of our taxi we saw a Brahman cow, a great big hump-back thing, tied to a stake by the side of the road so we decided that we would have ride. We undid it from the stake and for the next ten minutes tried to mount it but it was not very happy about that and finished up galloping off down the road. We did not see it again but unfortunately the cow had been covered in shit and, consequently, so were we. We were refused entry to three separate brothels on account of smelling so bad so we returned home to the Great Eastern Hotel, had a shower and went to bed.

I joined the squadron the next morning and met 'Bush' Cotton and all the boys with an awful hangover. Meanwhile, Johnny Redman had joined Wingate's first expedition of Chindits, behind the lines, and I never saw him again because he crossed the Irrawaddy river going out, but got caught in a current and drowned when coming back. It was a great pity, because he was a 'bonza' chap. At that time, I was not a very good choice as a Flight Commander. I was bolshie because by now I hated the country. I thought I should never have been there and wanted to be back in England flying fighters again, not these awful, slow, old tank-busting Hurricanes with no tanks to bust and so I was not in the best of moods when I joined 17 Squadron. We were based at a big convent about three or four miles from the actual Red Road itself where I spent my time drinking more than anything else.

I owned a radiogram that I had bought at Dum Dum the HMV factory, a 12-volt battery and a great collection of records, Artie Shaw and all the good bands. One night a few of us got drunk on Pernod and we sat on the floor and threw all my records into the overhead fan. The next morning, when I came down with a terrible hangover, I realised what I had done. One could not see the actual floor; it was covered in black broken records. There must have been hundreds of Rupees worth of records. Those are the stupid things that I did at that time. I just hated the country and the food was awful. I was no good to myself or anybody else. I only lasted about three-and-a-half months with the squadron, doing operations down over Don Baik and where the army was fighting the Japanese in the Arakan. When we weren't up there we were back at Red Road. It was a funny sort of situation. During the three-and-a-half months

I spent with them, we got up to all sorts of high jinks. While we were in Calcutta we used to fly local and it was CO's great love to fly in close formation all the time. Having been through France and the Battle of Britain, I knew that tight formation was not the thing at all; you had to fly in loose formation, so you could keep an eye open for the enemy. The CO had come out from Australia, and gone straight to 17 Squadron in Burma, and had no experience of flying in Europe at all. He was not prepared to listen so we did not see eye-to-eye from the beginning.

While we were there we went down to a place called 'Reindeer' which was a flattened out paddy field south of Cox's Bazaar. We operated there for two to three weeks helping the Army, who had got themselves into trouble at a place called Don Baik where they were surrounded by the Japanese. We did a few operations down there, completely wasted as far as I could see, because all we shot up were bullock carts, I didn't see many Japanese at all.

Back at the Red Road, the Sergeant Pilots got their pay one morning and we decided to have a bit of fun. I had a *Crown and Anchor* board so I took it round to the Dispersal Hut there and we played *Crown and Anchor*. Of course I was the banker and I finished up winning a thousand rupees. Not a great amount of money, but it was a thousand rupees nonetheless, and I had a tip for a racehorse called Steamroller I put the whole lot as an each way bet on Steamroller for a race that was due to be run that afternoon when I was flying. The racecourse was practically next-door to the Red Road, so when I came in to land, I circled the racecourse. Knowing that my jockey was wearing an emerald green silk, I could see that he was at the back of the field when they came into the straight and he finished nowhere. After that I put my wheels down, flaps down and came in to land. It was a hot afternoon and there were birds, Kite hawks, over the end of the runway and I had to go through them. I seemed to be going very fast when I touched down, halfway down the Red Road, and I was still doing about 80 mph. I kept going until I was nearly towards the end of the road where there was a bamboo fence cutting the Red Road off from the rest of Calcutta. There must have been a thousand people watching me coming straight towards them and they were not moving – not the least bit worried! I got to within 100 yds of them, realised that I was not going to stop, so I put on full left rudder and brake and did a ground loop. I went straight round and hit a statue of Lord Roberts, knocked a lump of concrete off his plinth and did a bit of damage to the aircraft wing. When I got out, the CO was not at all pleased with me because, in the excitement of watching the race, I had selected my wheels down twice, and landed without any flaps. So, once again, I was in the CO's bad books

About three days later the whole squadron moved down to a field south of Calcutta on the Hooghly River called 'Acorn'. It was while there, after having had a few drinks on a beautiful moonlit night, that I and a New Zealand Sergeant Pilot decided it would be lovely to fly. So, we went out to the aircraft and, of course, we told the Flight Sergeant in charge of aircraft and engines, who tried to stop us but knew he was wasting his time, so he got the CO. The CO came down and put a stop to it straight away and put me under open-arrest. The next day I was sent to Calcutta to 221 Group and never went back to the squadron. A couple of days later I was marched up before Air Commodore Fullergood who used to be our CO at Crosby-on-Eden. He gave me a severe reprimand and a loss of six months' seniority and I was posted to 151 OTU Risalpur. The following day I went to collect all goods and chattels in my tin trunk that I had put in the Army and Navy Stores about a year before. I then went into The Great Eastern Hotel to have a drink and who should I meet there but Mike Hunt. He used to be with us at Perth when we first did our training in Scotland. He was in the Volunteer Reserve. We got together and there was very little to drink but Creme de Menthe so we finished up drinking a couple of bottles of that between us that morning. We then went out to Howra Station together in the afternoon to get my train. I was absolutely blind drunk by then; I got on the train and ended up having a fight with the MPs because I had not got a compartment on my own. Anyway, I finished up with a compartment to myself and off we went. I slept on a bunk and had the carriage windows open. Leaving Howra to cross India you went through lots and lots of tunnels before you got out into the open country and all the soot from the tunnels came in through my window and I woke up in the morning covered in soot and feeling like death warmed up. I then went to the toilet and I peed a bright green.

Chapter 18

Risalpur

After a three day train journey we arrived at Risalpur, which was an Air Force and Army Cantonment between Peshawar and Rawalpindi up in the North West Province of India. We were met at the station and taken to the mess. It was a peacetime station so at last we were in a decent mess after all the horrible and terrible conditions that we had been living in. The CO of the station was a Group Captain Darley who had been CO of 609 Squadron in the Battle of Britain, and the Chief Flying Officer was a Canadian called Hiram-Smith, who also had been in the Battle of Britain. I was made 'B' Flight Commander, which astounded me because I didn't think they would make me a Flight Commander after what had happened. The aircraft were Hurricanes and Harvards. We had to give dual instruction in the Harvards and solo in Hurricanes. It was just like an OTU, they flew in formation with you, and you led the pupils, most of whom were Indian. There were also a few western pilots converting to Hurricanes from other aircraft. It was a very hot summer so we would fly from dawn until about 9 or 10 am and then we would pack up and spend our day at the swimming pool or under fans and punkers in the mess and start flying again about 4 pm until dark. It was so hot that I burnt my hands once when trying to get into the aircraft without gloves, putting my hands on the side of the plane

This carried on until September when I contracted a very high temperature and was sent to hospital. When I got there they pricked me and tried to find malaria. They also took my blood but they could not find anything wrong. My temperature kept on going up and eventually they discovered I had Dengue Fever. Every time I moved my eyes, even slightly, I got a terrible headache. I also had heat-stroke so they treated me for that but still could not get my temperature down. The next night I had a rubber blanket around me with lots of ice in it and they were sticking a thermometer up my bottom every five minutes to get my temperature and kept pricking my finger. At last they found malaria and they dosed me up with quinine while my temperature was getting to the stage where they thought I was going to die. Within twenty-four hours it went right down to normal again. They told me afterwards that they did not know what they were going to do because I seemed to be thriving at a temperature of 109°F! Anyway, they placed me on this German drug called Pamaquine, and I had to take one tablet a day but wasn't allowed any alcohol. I was in hospital so it did not make much difference. As I lay there on the Sunday, in came a bunch of boys from Risalpur to see how I was. They had bought a human skull from the Bazaar with them and since there were no nurse around on account of it being Sunday afternoon, I got up, got dressed and we stacked my bed with clothes, plumped it up, put the skull on my pillow and we all went to the railway station, which was the only place we could get beer on a Sunday. We sat there drinking beer even though I was not supposed to be drinking, when two MPs appeared who marched me smartly back to the hospital. When I got back there the Colonel gave me a dressing-down because it was a military hospital, and refused to have me in the hospital anymore. So I had to go back to my bungalow at the aerodrome.

While I was in hospital I met a Canadian by the name of Nicholson and he had a disease called Sprue. Basically you eat your food and it comes out the other end the same as it goes in and there seemed to be no cure for it. They told him that they would not let him out of hospital until he gave them at least one decent stool so I got together with him and said I'd give him a decent stool. When his doctor came round and inspected this stool they let him out. However, within two days he was back again and they finished up sending him home to Canada because they couldn't treat him at all. Apparently, it cured itself with a change of environment.

As soon as I had recovered from my illness I was sent on three weeks' leave. Four of us went to Srinigar: the engineer officer, myself and another couple of pilots. We went up by train to Rawalpindi and from there we got the bus to Srinigar which is the capital of Kashmir. It is about 150 to 200 miles by road through the Himalayas. You climb up to the highest point at about 8,000 ft through a place called Murree, a place well known for brewing beer, about forty miles from Rawalpindi. Then you just weave your way through the mountains until you get to a lush, beautiful valley which looks very much like scenery from Switzerland, with walnut trees everywhere. We stayed on a houseboat called the *Neine Bar* for three weeks there and had a wonderful time. It was an absolutely beautiful climate and lovely weather; it was one of the few times I enjoyed myself while in India. I went for a ride on a horse; I had never ridden a horse before and I was trotting along, feeling most uncomfortable, going carefully along a path with a big drop one side when it started to gallop. I did not know what to do, so I let go of the reins, hung on to his neck and kicked him; I was really scared stiff until he pulled up. When I got off I looked over the edge of the great drop that I could have fallen down, walked him back to where I got him from and I have never been on a horse since!

Chapter 19

9IAF Squadron, Bhopal

February 1944

At the end of three weeks, when I got back to Risalpur, I found that I had been attached to Peshawar, which was a short flight away. I didn't know what I was supposed to do there but they just wanted to get rid of me because I was still playing up and my little episode in hospital didn't help either. I went there at the end of October where I teamed up with an Australian by the name of Salas and we got along like a house on fire. He was the pilot for the AOC, who was based there and used to fly him around in an Anson. We used to live in the same bungalow together and one night we both got absolutely rotten drunk. We went back to our room and had one hell of a fight; we smashed nearly all the furniture, which was all rented. We finished up the next day having to replace it, and pay for it. While I was there I got attached to Kohat, which was over the mountains, where I played tennis and cricket and enjoyed myself thoroughly. I also met up again with Flight Lieutenant Henry who had been our intelligence officer for 253 Squadron in France and during the Battle of Britain. We played tennis and cricket together, and then I went back to Peshawar. On 20 January 1944, I was posted to 113 Squadron at Dimapur, which is the railhead at Assam, an awful place; absolutely riddled with mosquitoes and malaria in the lowlands down by the Brahmaputra. I thought to myself, "Oh my God, here we go again". Anyway, I left Risalpur and got to Dimapur by train and boat. I was only there for three days when me and two

Canadians by the name of Hart and Butler were all sent or posted to 9 Indian Air Force Squadron, which was at Bhopal in central India. Hart was absolutely mad, I am quite sure of that. We all made our way to Bhopal via Calcutta, where we stayed for three days.

We arrived at 9IAF Squadron in February 1944 and flew around locally having a great time. The Nawabs of Bhopal had lots of yachts on the lake and allowed us to go sailing when we weren't flying. It was all very pleasant but I knew it couldn't last of course, and on 23 March we were sent to Kalora in Assam, because they were expecting some movement from the Japanese. We were also going to invade Burma. Kalora was just an old tea-garden with basha huts and the same old charpoys, full of bugs, dirt floor and we had a bar which was built of bamboo.

We were given money by the Central Fund at 221 Group in Calcutta to buy grog so that we could have a drink there. It was a funny sort of a set-up. We were only there for a short while before they sent us to Amarda Road, south of Calcutta, on a tactics course which was run by Frank Carey, an excellent pilot and veteran of the Battle of Britain. We were there for two to three weeks, during which one of our pilots had a heart attack and died. I still have the photographs of his funeral in my album. The next thing we were back to Kalora. The Japanese had invaded Imphal and were coming through to Kohima. We were used on shooting up to help the Army but in dense jungle it was very difficult to see what we were shooting at. We didn't meet enemy fighters or anything like that, it was just attacking ground fire, which we couldn't really see anyway. I don't think any of us ever got hit. While we were there we drank our entire ration and didn't have anything left so we decided that the best way to get more money out of the Group was to burn the Mess down, which is what we did. I'm afraid I was the culprit. I started the fire and it got out that I was responsible, although everybody else was in on it too. Unfortunately it set fire to a few other huts too and that night we all had to sleep out in the open, hoping it would not rain until they had built new huts for us in the morning. We were given another grant by Group to get some more grog so Butler, one of the Canadians, flew down to Calcutta in a Harvard and loaded it up with cases of liquor and took a bottle of gin in the cockpit with him. The next thing we heard, he had force-landed about 100 miles away. He had consumed too much gin in the cockpit, got lost, and landed in a paddy field with the wheels up. So we had to go out and pick him up and pick all the grog up in a truck and bring it back.

Shortly after that, my sins caught up with me again and I was posted to the War Room at 224 Group at Chittagong. I made my way down from there on 6 June 1944 and was there until the 1 December, when I volunteered for a job, a Visual Control Point. This meant that you were attached to an Airborne Division. I had to go up to Chaklala, near Rawalpindi, to do five parachute jumps with a couple of friends: Johnny O'Mant, and D.Y. Reece. We had first met at 224 Group and became great friends. We got to Chaklala and went through the jumping course. For two weeks we did all the practices, swinging on ropes and jumping off high walls and all the things you were supposed to do. It was just before Christmas when we made our first two jumps. I got into the aircraft with a load of Ghurkas, about thirty of us, and they asked if I would mind going last. I went down the length of the aircraft, shuffling along, one, two, three, four while they were pushing them out, one by one. By the time I got to the door after all thirty of them had gone, there were thirty straps hanging out and I could barely get through the door. I was pushed out of the plane and the next thing, the chute was open and it was wonderful. The feeling of coming down by parachute was great, I really enjoyed it. After two trial jumps, we jumped with baggage on the end of long ropes, so that we could land with stores and things like that.

After this it was Christmas, which was one of the funniest Christmases I have ever spent in my whole life. We stayed in Rawalpindi, a very nice town compared with other Indian towns, one of the better ones. They had a Masonic Hall there, it was a peacetime Army station and very pleasant. This particular Christmas we got together on Christmas Eve and got very merry. Johnny and myself then woke up Christmas morning with a hangover from the night before. We then had a good breakfast and immediately started drinking again. At some time in the morning we decided to pay a visit to the Sergeants' Club in town and, on our way through the local markets, we bought a live duck and immediately christened it Donald. We tied a long piece of string around its neck and it accompanied us for the rest of the day. We arrived at the Sergeants' Club and teamed up with a few of our jumping mates, who were already well under the weather, and one or two ladies. Some of these fellows were stationed there on a permanent basis and had their wives with them. One of these Sergeants had a small brown bear, it was on a lead tied to a post and seemed very quiet and contented. After a while we decided to move onto the Masonic Club, and we were arranging who to take as partners when one of the very 'merry' men slapped the bear on the back and said, "I'll take the lady in the fur coat", whereupon the bear turned around and bit him! We thought that was hilarious since he was not feeling much pain at the time.

The day progressed in much the same manner; all of us feeding Donald with small amounts of alcohol, we found that he was quite partial to Creme de Menthe so that when we finally got back to the mess we placed Donald on the Bar counter and found that one of his legs had collapsed so that he continually went round in circles until he fell off the Bar, whereupon he was replaced and the saga continued. Finally we went to bed taking Donald with us. In the morning we woke up with a room full of duck shit, terrible hangovers and a drunken duck, which I can assure you was a sight to behold. Donald had become our friend and it was impossible to kill him so we gave him to the Sergeant's Mess. The result of that day was a tremendous bruise that I had down the side of my leg from the top of my thigh to my kneecap. I had inflicted this on myself the day before by continually acting out my party trick of standing on one leg and kicking myself over with the other on concrete floors! I might say that it took a month of physiotherapy and great pain to bring the bruise out and I could not continue my jumps until it was finished.

Chapter 20

Black Watch Regiment, Secunderabad

February 1945

After completing my jumps I was posted to the First Battalion of the Black Watch Regiment at Secunderabad at the beginning of February. I went down to join them by train via Delhi and saw the Taj Mahal at Agra for the first time. I got to Secunderabad and reported to the CO, who was Colonel McKenzie. He welcomed me and at the same time informed me that the Battalion was going on a twenty-odd mile route march the following day and I should go to stores and get a good pair of boots. You could have knocked me over with a feather. I informed the Colonel that I did not intend to go on any route march.

Within twenty-four hours I was posted to a Field Howitzer Brigade, also in Secunderabad. They had these little Howitzers that were dropped by parachute. They looked like toy guns but were quite deadly. I packed up my gear and joined them and met the CO. This was a much better posting, as the CO loved aeroplanes and took all the magazines about flying; he also had wanted to join the RAF. He took me under his wing and I went on all their exercises. We used to go out into the field and fire on targets three or four miles away. I took part in *Map Reading for Direction and Elevation of Guns* and I found it was very interesting. While I was in Secunderabad the war in Europe ceased, so we had a great celebration. We lived in a Mess with some old field-guns from the Indian Mutiny outside the gates. We filled them up with Howitzer charges and set fire to them. We also had a great bonfire – it was a very fiery night! After that I was sent on a Battle Course for one week. It was very hot, temperatures were up in the hundreds and I'm sure I must have lost 15 lbs on that course. During the day we were put in trenches and fired at by twenty-five pounders, plus great charges of explosives by the edge of the trench, which were detonated at intervals. There was also an exercise where we had to attack another troop at dawn, so we marched at night in the pouring rain. I was part of a 2-inch mortar crew and had to carry two packs of six mortar bombs. We walked for some miles carrying these damned things through the freezing rain until we reached the point where we were to attack. I didn't get a second of sleep, but stayed awake all night trying to keep warm and when the dawn finally came, we made our attack. During the attack we fired off most of our mortar shells but I got left with one carrier full of six shells which I would have had to carry all the way back so I thought 'to Hell with that' and I hid them under a boulder. I've often wondered if anyone has ever found them.

Around this time we found out that we were training for Operation Zipper, which was an airborne invasion of Singapore. We were going to invade Malaysia, just north of the island of Singapore. The next thing we knew, the whole unit was moved to Bilaspur which was in the central provinces of India, it was sticky, humid and nowhere near as nice a place as Secunderabad. Bilaspur was a railway centre run mostly by Anglo-Indians who used to run the railways. We camped in tents and bamboo huts. I spent most of the week we were there shooting pye-dogs which were invading the camp (terrible dogs, all scabs and open sores, so they had to go). I was told we were going to be doing Combined Operations at a place called Cocanada, just North of Madras, which was about 800 miles south-east from us. It was decided that I would take a Jeep with three paratroopers with me. We took off in this Jeep and had the most marvellous scenic trip over the Eastern Ghats, terrific country. We stayed the first night at Oak Bungalow at the top of the hills. We had taken eggs, chicken, corn beef and stuff like that, so we had no problem with food. The birdlife was absolutely wonderful. It was thick jungle, mountainous country. Off we went the next morning, our next stop being Vizagapatam. We were going down a long straight road with trees on each side, which were full of Gibbons with great big long arms and they all had little babies with them. They jabbered and chattered as we drove along, and we hoped they wouldn't attack us because there were hundreds of them. It was a wonderful sight. Fortunately, they stayed up in the trees jabbering and chattering and we went through safely. We finished up at Vizag that night, but there was nowhere to stay so we slept on a table in the railway station and were eaten alive by mosquitoes. We couldn't wait to get out of there quick enough so first thing in the morning we were off again. We arrived at Cocanada the next day but were only there for a couple of days and didn't get to see much of the combined exercise. We set off on our return journey the next day and it took us another two-and-a-half to three days to get back. Altogether it had been a wonderful trip although a little uncomfortable.

Chapter 21

Force 136, Colombo, Ceylon

September 1945

Shortly after that the war finished against Japan when the Atomic Bomb was dropped and, in September, I was posted to Colombo in Ceylon to join Force 136. Force 136 were the cloak-and-dagger people who had been behind the lines in France and other places throughout the world during the war. I was supposed to be dropping into the Prisoner of War Camps in Java and Sumatra with other agents and radios, but when we finally joined Force 136 HQ just south of Colombo, a bamboo hut camp on the edge of a swamp, they found out that Sukarno was taking over everything. This was against the plans of the British and Dutch Governments, so they decided they didn't have the planes to drop the RAF in; they would drop more troops in instead and so we finished up staying down at Force 136 doing nothing. Nothing to do but drink and go into Colombo spending our days at the Mount Lavinia Hotel, swimming and drinking – but of course our pay wouldn't run to that so we ran out of money and we had to stay in the camp, which soon became deadly monotonous.

There was one relief however, we had quite a few FANYs (First Aid Nursing Yeomanry) and we used to take them out and carouse with them, I had an affair with one, so that part was quite good. But, of course, our money would not run to it all the time, so we got up to mischief. It was somebody's birthday before too long and the grog ration had just come in; we had been short of it for about three days and had not had a drink. The officer in charge would not give us our ration until the next day so we broke in and took our grog ration, leaving them payment on the counter. We went back and got very drunk. I had a habit at the time of setting fire to things when I was drunk so when I got very mad with this particular fellow, I ended up setting fire to the settee in the Mess and before we knew it, the whole hut went up in flames and set fire to a few others too. I finished up under arrest and a Summary of Evidence was taken. They took the Summary of Evidence very quickly next day because all these agents, Force 136, were going into different parts of South East Asia. No-one's evidence was the same as anybody else's. They were all on my side because they were behind it as much as I was – except I lit the actual fire. When it was all over two days later, it was decided that everybody had committed perjury so they had to hold the whole Summary of Evidence again. By that time however, one person was in England, two or three others were in Borneo and Sumartra, – they were spread all over the world – so it was decided to scrap the whole thing and I was posted with two of my RAF friends, Bob Dodds and Lyons, to the Air force Base at Ratmalana in Colombo.

That was no good to us because all we did at Ratmalana was stay at the Camp with absolutely nothing to do, so we ended up drinking again. We got extremely drunk on Christmas Eve and entertained everybody; we had been drinking all day so by nighttime we were quite inebriated and I started to break the Mess up and did several stupid things. I was told to go to bed and I refused so I was put under arrest. The next day I woke up in my bed with no memory of what had gone on the day before. There were two other officers in my room and when I asked what was going on, they informed me that I was under close-arrest. So, that was that. When under close-arrest, the escorts are not supposed to leave you, there should be at least one escort with you at all times. These two bods went up to the Mess and left me behind in the room. I thought, 'to Hell with this' and off I trooped into Colombo. I went and saw *For Whom the Bell Tolls* by Ernest Hemingway with Gary Cooper and Ingrid Bergman. When I got back the whole camp was in an uproar all looking for me. They thought I had escaped so I was in trouble again, but I was in so much trouble it did not matter then. I was fed up with India because the War was over and I was still there; all I wanted to do was to be dismissed from the Service and get out. I had had enough. I had had nearly four years living like a pig without one home leave.

Chapter 22

130 Squadron, RAF Odiham, England

August 1946

I finished up going up to Kandy and being Court Martialled for 'Conduct Prejudicial to Good Conduct Discipline' or whatever it is they charged you with. I was found guilty, given a severe reprimand and a loss of two years seniority. So, back to Ratmalana I went. As soon I got back, Dodds, Lyons and me were posted to our unit which was then up on the North West frontier; a vineyard near Rawlpindi. We had only been there about a week when I got my posting back to England. I was flown down to Karachi and there boarded a Liberator Bomber, which had been transformed – they had put seats in the bomb bay and turned it into a sort of passenger aircraft. It was a most uncomfortable trip, sitting in the bomb bay. I was sitting with an army Captain by the name of Bushell – his brother, Anthony Bushell, was a film star who I had seen in films – we got talking and got on quite well together. It was a ten-hour trip from Karachi to Cairo, where we stayed over night. It was then an eight-hour trip in the bomb bay to Tripoli where we spent a night and a day.

We took off the following day but no sooner had we taken off with a full-load of fuel to go straight back to England than one of the motors played up then cut out, so they had to return and land with this full load of fuel. It was a most dicey landing, which took up the full length of Castel Benito's three-mile-long runway. We ended up spending another four days in Tripoli which, at that time, was a Harbour full of sunken ships with nothing to sell in the shops but sponges. While we were there, the British Government had given a time limit to return old five pound notes because they were going to issue new ones because the Germans had printed and distributed millions of the old notes. The storekeepers had lots of these old notes and, knowing they would become worthless within a few days, were exchanging a pound for five pounds. When we got back to England however, we knew that our notes would be cashed for us because we had been in transit so we did quite nicely out of that!

When we took off again four days later we got as far as France when the weather closed in over Cambridge where we were going to land, so we had to make another stop and found ourselves in Bordeaux. There was no accommodation ready for us in Bordeaux so we ended up spending the night in a brothel. We took some girls and spent all night touring Bordeaux. The fun fair was going and we had a really good night.

The next day we were off again and finally landed at Cambridge. Home at last! After just over four years, I was so glad to be back. Being February, it was cold and dreary, but it was wonderful after India. While I had been away, my parents had moved into a big block of flats near Richmond in Surrey, so I went back there. We renewed acquaintances and I decided that I would have a tour of England. I had been in touch with Jack Strang, a New Zealander who had been in 253 Squadron so we got together and toured England for a couple of weeks. We went all around the place enjoying ourselves until I was posted to Tangmere, West Sussex in May. This was non-flying and I was appointed Fire Officer and Sports Officer. As Fire Officer, I organised the Fire Station and training exercises; keeping all in readiness for an emergency. As Sports Officer, I organised a cricket team and we played other stations at cricket. I loved cricket, having played for my School 1st Eleven and also in India. Eventually,

I finished up playing for 11 Group and Fighter Command. I remember we got to the Finals in the RAF; Fighter Command met Bomber Command at Surrey Oval. It was a rotten day, raining off and on, typical English summer. Batting at number seven, I walked all the way out to the centre, took my guard, was bowled first ball, then walked all the way back. It was a long walk! I did take a couple of wickets though.

While at Tangmere I had an affair with the Senior WAAF officer there, Molly Dee, who was a lovely girl and we used to go around together all the time, until eventually I was posted to 130 Squadron at Odiham for flying duties; I was very happy. When I arrived at Odiham they were flying Spitfire MkIX's and I flew with them for a month. The CO was 'Buck' Courtney who, funnily enough, was the CO of 113 Squadron where I had been posted in India. I had only stayed for a week before he posted me back to No.9 Indian Squadron. It was quite amusing to find him there, I thought he'd want rid of me at the first opportunity, but he was very fair and I lasted three months before I was posted. We flew Spit 9's before being equipped with de Havilland Vampire jets. We were the second squadron to be equipped with Vampires and they were wonderful to fly but my first trip was quite nerve wracking. We had a session to familiarise ourselves with the cockpit and so on, but you could not fly dual. When you took off in the Vampire, you pulled a lever (with your hood closed) and it put air in the cushion between the hood and the fuselage so that it was airtight and you could not hear any noises from outside. I remember taking off and, as I got airborne, I pulled this lever and suddenly there was no noise at all. I thought my engine had cut so I put the nose down and was looking for a place to land before I realised that the engine was still going well and it was just this cushion that had filled with air, cutting out the engine noise!

Chapter 23

33 Squadron, Fassberg, Germany

November 1946

I was with 130 Squadron from August until November when I was posted to33 Squadron at Fassberg in Germany where they were flying Tempest II's. I said goodbye to 130 Squadron and caught the ferry over to the entrance to the Kiel Canal, then by train down to Celle, near Luneberg Plain, there I was met by a truck and taken up to the station at Fassberg about twenty miles from Celle. I arrived late at night, it was very dark and very cold with snow everywhere. I entered this beautiful Mess and went to the Bar where there were two Senior Officers – one of whom was Johnny Johnson and, down the other end, three young officers who were making a lot of noise. They were drunk and being stupid like young officers usually are at that age, so Johnny Johnson went down to them and said, "If you can't behave like gentlemen please go to your bed". So, off they went to their beds. The strangest thing was that Johnny Johnson had not a stitch of clothing on him; he was completely naked. That was my initiation into Fassberg.

I enjoyed my time there, we did a lot of flying. There were two other squadrons of Tempest II's but we were the only operational rocket-wing flying with the Air Force at the time so we used to go back and forth from Germany to Salisbury Plain in England; doing exercises with the Army like tank-busting, then head back to Germany. While we were in England we used to fill up with coffee, you could walk to within 10 yards of one of these planes and smell the coffee. Coffee was a great commodity in Germany, you could get anything for it – radios, cameras, anything you liked. We used to fly under the bridges down the Kiel Canal,–they were very high bridges, so it was not much to fly under them and we used to get up to mischief too. Lubeck is a great seaside place for the Germans on the Baltic and they used to have these high bamboo sort of shelters which they would use as shade from the sun; we used to dive down on them and pull up steeply to try to blow them over with the slip-stream – until we got reported. At the same time I had a steady girlfriend whom I had met in Hamburg. At weekends, she worked for the BAFO (British Air Forces of Occupation) and every weekend, or nearly every weekend, I used to go up and meet her.

Other weekends, when we didn't go into Hamburg, we would organise a hunting party and we would go out shooting deer and wild boar. The German hunters were not allowed to have rifles so they acted as the beaters and they had longhaired Dachshunds. We used to go out to pine forests. They were all in squares with a lane running between them, about 10 ft wide and we would put ourselves round three sides of a square while the beaters went through the other side with their dogs. We would be at about one hundred yards intervals with our rifles. I remember hearing a noise one day, like an express train coming through. Suddenly, about 200 massive boars came screaming towards us, only about 10 yards from me, straight across the road. I didn't have time to fire at them; I was frightened as much as anything because when you wound a boar, you have to go in after it, but they are the most dangerous creatures to go in after because they just lie in wait and then attack you. I didn't fire at any of them just in case I ended up wounding one, because they were going too fast. We couldn't have gone in after them; the Beaters would have had to go in for them. Still, I got a very nice deer, a big buck, and I was blooded. At the end of the evening we all got into the back of the truck with the dead animals, less their livers, which had been removed. Then we went to the local inn, where we ate Saukraut and liver and drank Schnapps. We had some hilarious times. The German hunters were very friendly. Because most of them had come by bicycle, on the way back, we would take their bicycles on the back of the truck and drop them off, one by one. Also, during that time, the whole wing did an exercise at Oldenburg. So we all flew to Oldenburg and there we had a week doing all sorts of things.

In July of 1947, I decided that I wouldn't stay on in the Air Force. I knew that if I did, I would do very little flying. From then on I would be on Courts of Enquiry and Courts Martial, probably finishing up on the wrong side of the bench in a Court Martial myself, so I decided it was time to get out. In July I was posted back to England to be demobbed. The night before I left Fassberg, I laid on a big party for everyone in the Mess. It did not cost much, because liquor in Germany was so very cheap. You could get a bottle of liquor for six shillings a bottle, whereas beer was almost as expensive. I left early the following morning and flew in to Blackpool where I was demobbed. I spent the night there and went out on the town, met another fellow there and we had a bit of a night together. Next morning I collected my civilian clothes and was paid off.

I caught the train back to Richmond and that was the end of my career in the RAF, except that I was then placed on the Reserve; meaning that for the next few years, I had to spend two weeks during the summer at Fairoaks flying Tiger Moths, which was great fun.

I would not have missed my eight-and-a-half years' service. I went through some terrible times I also had some wonderful times. My downfall, of course, was alcohol. During my service I received a reprimand, severe reprimand, and a Court Martial, all because I had drunk too much. It's unfortunate that, when under the 'alfuence of inkahol' I didn't pass out like most people, or stagger around the place; it didn't show. Instead, I used to drink, talk plainly and end up doing the most outrageous things. I can understand now why I got into such trouble so I can't really complain.

My dealings with the Air Force had not quite finished because, some months later, I received a letter from the Air Ministry. Apparently, there had been an 'oversight'. After I had been court martialled and lost two years seniority, accounts had failed to reduce my pay accordingly and I owed, I don't know what the exact figure was now, but it ran into a few thousand pounds and I was expected to send it to them! You can imagine what I did – I just tore the letter up and threw it away.

A few weeks' later, I received another letter, exactly the same. They were not threatening me in any way, just asking for it to be returned, so I threw it away again. I never heard another thing from them, which is just as well because I did not have any money to pay them, only my gratuity. I had no intention of paying them anyway. It serves them right, I should never have been court martialled in the first place!

Chapter 24

Lest We Forget

No.253 Squadron RAF

CODE LETTERS: SW
Battle of Britain Aircraft: Hawker Hurricane

BATTLE OF BRITAIN AIRFIELDS:
Reformed Manston: October 30, 1939
Northolt: February 14, 1940 to May 8, 1940
Kenley: May 8, 1940 to May 24, 1940, with detachment to Poix, France
Kirton-in-Lindsey: May 24 to July 21, with detachment to Coleby
    Grange and Ringway, 1940
Prestwick: May 29, 1940 – August 29th 1940
Kenley: August 29, 1940 to January 3, 1941

Aircrew who served with No.253 squadron during the Battle of Britain

F/Sgt K.M.Allen
F/Sgt H.H.Allgood
Sgt J.A.Anderson
P/O A.R.H.Barton
P/O D.B.Bell-Salter
P/O E.G.Bidgood
S/L E.R.Bitmead

F/O G.A.Brown
F/L W.P.Cambridge
P/O G.C.T.Carthew
Sgt I.C.C.Clenshaw
P/O J.K.G.Clifton
Sgt S.F.Cooper
P/O A.H.Corkett

Sgt V.E.Cukr

Sgt J.H.Dickinson

Sgt A.S.Dredge

S/L R.M.B.D.Duke-Woolley

F/O A.E.Eckford

F/L G.R.Edge

Sgt A.Edgley

P/O C.D.Francis

S/L T.P.Gleave

P/O R.C.Graves

P/O J.P.B.Greenwood

P/O D.J.Hammond

Sgt W.B.Higgins

Sgt R.A.Innes

P/O D.N.O.Jenkins

Sgt E.R.Jessop

Sgt E.H.C.Kee

S/L E.B.King

Sgt S.Kita

Sgt M.Kopecky

P/O G.Marsland

Sgt J.Metham

Sgt P.J.Moore

P/O L.C.Murch

P/O T.Nowak

F/O S.R.Peacock-Edwards

P/O D.A.Pennington

P/O W.M.C.Samolinski

S/L H.M.Starr

F/O J.T.Strang

P/O A.A.G.Trueman

F/L R.E.Watts

F/L J.H.Wedgwood

Sgt R.O.Whitehead

P/O D.S.Yapp

Epilogue

Released from the RAF in 1947, and with his youth gone, John tried to settle down in post-war London. His younger sister and great friend, Ruth, had met an American officer during the war who she went on to marry. They raised three children together, Melody, David and Peter. Most of their childhood was spent in Kenya. Ruth passed away in 1981 and Peter was tragically killed in a peace-time helicopter accident while serving with the US Navy in 1990. John's older sister, Betty, married an ex-Battle of Britain pilot, raising two children, Mary Ann and Alec, in the tranquil surrounds of rural Scotland. She passed away in 2008.

In 1950, John and a friend boarded a ship from Southampton bound for Australia, the best move of his life. On arrival, he worked many odd jobs throughout this wild and wonderful country. Finally, he joined the airline industry as a pilot. It was here that he formed many close friendships and met an airline hostess, Joyce Tomlinson, whom he married in 1954.

They left the airlines and settled in Perth for a short time, prior to an eleven-year stint running their own business and raising four children in the Western Australian country town of Gnowangerup. The children: Helen, Christopher, Michael and Nicholas all enjoyed the experience of growing up in a rural environment.

In 1973, the Greenwoods moved back to Perth and in 1981, John retired and led an interesting and active life in good health and humour until he passed away on 31 December 2014 at the age of ninety-three.

Postscript

John wrote his manuscript over 20 years ago. I learned of its existence in August 2014, through a mutual friend Pippa Ettore, who runs a Battle of Britain discussion forum, which John and other pilots contributed to, and offered to help edit it for publication. Over the next four months I sent chapters to John for comment. We also talked on the 'phone about what he had written, his experiences during the war and life in general. With the help of John's wife Joyce, we were able to put together a first draft, which she was able to give him a few days after he went into hospital in the week prior to Christmas. Sadly, John passed away on New Year's Eve 2014. As a mark of respect, the family organised for a condolence book on line. The response to this was overwhelming with over 100 messages from people around the world. A number of these are printed below as a tribute to John, the pilots of 253 Squadron and the 'Few'. Subsequently, with help from Joyce and Mike Greenwood and Dean Sumner with additional material from the Shoreham Aircraft Museum and Lee Brimmicombe-Wood, we put together a second draft for publication.

Mark Nottle
Bibaringa, July 2015.

Never before in the field of human conflict has so much been given to so many by so few. My sincere condolences.

Rest in Peace Sir – thank you for our freedom.

May God protect you, as protected us, rest in peace kind sir …

You and your comrades are absolute heroes and you will never be forgotten.

Thank you for your help in our hour of need. Rest in peace John.

We never met, but know that I will always, always remember you, and what you did for the world.

Thank you for your service for all of us.

John, Sir. Thank you for your service and the freedom we have today. May you always have blue skies and the wind on your tail. RIP, lest we Forget

You are the reason I am here, Sir. God bless you. Fly with the birds …

Thanks for the freedom which you won for my generation. My deepest gratitude to you and your mates.

To the memory of a man served in our hour of need to ensure that we have the freedom that we now enjoy – thank you.

There are no words to express my gratitude to you and your colleagues.

Our sincerest thanks to John for his bravery and dedication in our darkest hour.

We owe you so much, for what we have today, We will always remember .

John was there when the call to arms came in order to prevent the invasion of this country, the deeds and heroism carried out by John and his comrades will never be forgotten by those who are aware just how close Britain came to disaster. No words can ever describe the admiration I have for these gentlemen who are known ever more now as the few, they quite simply are legendary. Rest in peace John – per Ardua ad Astra.

Deepest respects for you John, I salute you sir for your courage & honour in defending the UK in our time of need to preserve our freedom. Long may the ethos of freedom be defended & protected. John, you & your comrades will never be forgotten, the Few will fly together for eternity in the heavens.

Thank you John, your life has gone down in history and millions owe their lives to you. Rest in Peace sir.

Rest now with your chums in the squadron. Lest we forget. Per ardua ad Astra.

Thank you John, one of Britain's hero's, in her hour of need, God Bless.

My deepest condolences for the sad passing of John. May he now rest with his fellow pilots.

A simple thank you.

Sir Winston Churchill said that we owed so much to so few. No truer word has ever been spoken since then! I personally thank you, all the pilots of the RAF and all the World War 2 veterans of allied forces alive or dead for my freedom.

Dear John,
God bless and thanks for your service to the nation. My father may have helped in vectoring you into action (on the radar) and he couldn't praise you guys higher!

Thank you for all what you did you will never be forgotten a real hero. A light to shine bright forever more

Soar forever upwards

Thanks, can't say anymore than that and it never seems enough

God speed and blue skies John and thank you for your service gone but not forgotten

RIP and Blue Skies …

Your duty is done; now it's time for rest. We are in your debt.

From another fighter pilot. Thank you for what you did Sir. God bless you

Another hero takes one last sortie to the skies, Rest in Peace Sir & thank you

From a fellow RAF pilot, God speed, John. Finally, your hard work has led you to the stars.

Rest in peace and thx for your effort and bravery. You don't know me but you guys are the reason I can live in peace and freedom in the Netherlands.

Farwell Fl/Lt Greenwood. R.I.P. and Blue Skies, Sir.

Thank you sir from a Kentish man who was privileged to see the bravery of the FEW.

Per Ardua Ad Astra our utmost thanks to you Rest in Peace Sir

May you, John, rest in peace forever. Your task is now done and you can now rejoin your fellow pilots!

Dear John and your family, I did not know you Sir, but I respect you totally for your service on our behalf. Thank you so much, God's speed & Blue skies. Chocks away. R.I.P old comrades await you.
Rest in peace John, thank you for serving in our armed forces and fighting so bravely LEST WE FORGET.

A simple "thank you" will never be adequate. You risked your all so that the world would know peace. God bless you sir.

Blue skies to you, John, as you join your heavenly squadron for your eternal flight … my condolences to your family and friends.

"We few, we happy few, we band of brothers."